M000281451

The Palmetto Trail Lowcountry Guide

Second Edition

Palmetto Conservation Foundation/ PCF Press

Sponsored by Santee Cooper

ISBN-10: 0-9745284-7-1
ISBN-13: 978-0-9745284-7-2

The authors and publisher have made every attempt to insure the accuracy of the information provided herein. However, they accept no responsibility for any loss, damage, injury or inconvenience sustained by any person using this book. Users of this book should be aware that wilderness travel carries certain inherent risks and can be dangerous or even fatal.

Text and Editing: Yon Lambert, Oliver Buckles
Maps drawn by: Steve Collum
Design and Production: Sandy Husmann and Susan Jones Ferguson
Cover photograph: James M. Huff

Printed in the USA

Library of Congress Cataloging-in-Publication Data

Lambert, Yon, 1971-
  The palmetto trail lowcountry guide. -- 2nd ed. / [text and editing, Yon Lambert, Oliver Buckles].
    p. cm.
  ISBN 978-0-9745284-7-2
  1. Hiking--South Carolina--Guidebooks. 2. Trails--South Carolina--Guidebooks. 3. Palmetto Trail--Guidebooks. 4. South Carolina--Guidebooks. I. Buckles, Oliver. II. Palmetto Conservation Foundation. III. Title.
  GV199.42.S58L36 2007
  796.5109756--dc22
                        2007042114

Acknowledgements

We dedicate this guidebook to Palmetto Trail's Lowcountry coordinator Oliver Buckles who has worked tirelessly to maneuver the trail across some unforgiving terrain.

A former U.S. Forest Service employee, Oliver came out of semi-retirement to assist with the planning and layout of the Palmetto Trail. He has since brokered numerous agreements with landowners, private citizens and large organizations alike. Where Oliver couldn't find a suitable route for the trail across open fields or forest, he pushed onward using some of the rural, dirt roads that crisscross the Lowcountry. Improvements to the trail are being made as new rights-of-way agreements are secured.

A passionate, adopted resident of the Lowcountry, Oliver also leads natural history tours of the trail. His knowledge of trail maintenance, plants, animals and the environment is encyclopedic, and his insight proved invaluable to this guide.

We can't thank him enough for all his hard work and time.

Palmetto Trail's Lowcountry coordinator Oliver Buckles leads a discussion about the Battle of Eutaw Springs.

Trail Notes

Help Us Keep This Guide Up to Date!

The authors and publisher have made every effort to make this guide as accurate and useful as possible. However, many things can change after a guide is published — phone numbers, addresses, etc...

Please inform us about your experience with this guide. While we may not be able to respond to all comments, we'll do the best we can and make certain to take them into consideration for the next edition of this guide or subsequent guides about the Palmetto Trail. Please send your comments and suggestions to:

Palmetto Conservation
1314 Lincoln St., Suite 305
Columbia, SC 29201
(803) 771-0870
www.palmettoconservation.org

CAUTION!

This book is intended only as a general guide to the Palmetto Trail and is not a substitute for individual outdoor skills, including survival and route finding. Each visitor to the Palmetto Trail should possess these outdoor skills or be accompanied by an individual who does. Palmetto Conservation and the authors assume no liability for accidents happening to, or injuries sustained by, readers who engage in activities described in this book.

Sunset on Lake Moultrie

Foreward

Dear Reader,

Welcome to the Lowcountry of South Carolina! This part of
the state is rich with natural beauty, and one of the best ways to
experience all that we have to offer is by traveling the Palmetto Trail.

The Palmetto Trail opened to great fanfare in 1996, with Santee Cooper's completion
of the 26-mile Lake Moultrie Passage. It created widespread access for hikers and
bicyclists to some of the most beautiful vistas around the lake it edges. Santee Cooper,
South Carolina's state-owned electric and water utility, was also instrumental in opening
two other passages around Eutaw Springs and Lake Marion.

This guidebook will help you navigate the 100-plus miles of Palmetto Trail winding
throughout the Lowcountry. It offers helpful tips on everything from weather to
amenities, and you'll also find sections on the history of each area. Eventually- when
the trail is complete-you will be able to hike or bike much farther, through the Midlands
and the Upstate, too.

Santee Cooper's primary responsibility is generating power for nearly 2 million South
Carolinians, including retail customers in Berkeley, Georgetown and Horry counties
and electric cooperative customers throughout the state. Our mission is to be the
leading resource for improving the lives of all South Carolinians. One way is promote
recreational use of the lakes that got us started in the power business: Lake Moultrie
and Lake Marion. These lakes have been popular fishing and boating destinations for
decades; the Palmetto Trail affords hikers and bicyclists another way to experience their
wonder.

Enjoy your journey through South Carolina's Lowcountry!

Sincerely,

Lonnie N. Carter
Santee Cooper President and Chief Executive Officer

Table of Contents

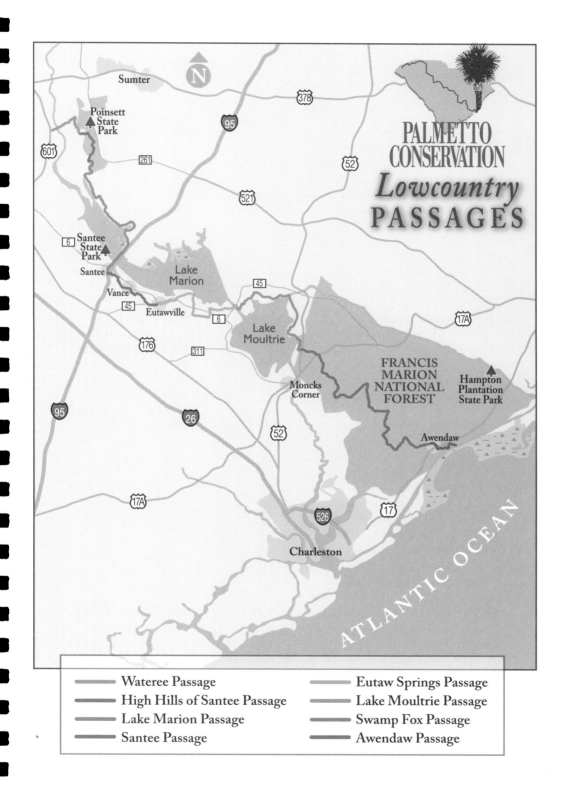

PALMETTO
CONSERVATION
Lowcountry
PASSAGES

Sumter

Poinsett
State
Park

Santee
State
Park

Santee

Vance

Eutawville

Lake
Marion

Lake
Moultrie

Moncks
Corner

FRANCIS
MARION
NATIONAL
FOREST

Hampton
Plantation
State Park

Awendaw

Charleston

ATLANTIC OCEAN

———— Wateree Passage
———— High Hills of Santee Passage
———— Lake Marion Passage
———— Santee Passage

———— Eutaw Springs Passage
———— Lake Moultrie Passage
———— Swamp Fox Passage
———— Awendaw Passage

Introduction

Hikers always seem to head for the hills. The same goes for mountain bikers and equestrians. In our wildest adventures, we're always doing something exotic like whitewater paddling in Peru, driving cattle through Wyoming or trekking in the Himalayas. Even here, on the East Coast, we're obsessed with our last wild places such as the rugged Blue Wall Escarpment or Jocassee Gorges. The grass was always greener there. ....*Until now.*

Now we have a long distance trail in South Carolina's Coastal Plain. But you may ask "Just where is the Coastal Plain?" The term is hard to define. People in the Upstate consider everything below Columbia as the Lowcountry. However, people along the coast have a more definitive answer and that being the Outer Coastal Plain. Some people define it by geography, others by the people, and some by the plants. Rice was the predominant crop of the Lowcountry during Colonial times and rice was grown from the coast all the way into the Wateree River floodplain. More likely the Lowcountry is a state of mind encompassing the entire Coastal Plain of South Carolina.

This guide is about rediscovering a region that's been South Carolina's front porch for 300 years: the Lowcountry. Like most familiar places, we sometimes fail to notice the beauty here. Only when we're actually out there do little things begin to accumulate. The way evening shadows from knobby bald cypress fade into inky creek water. Waking before dawn on the shores of Lake Marion to the hiss of a bass fisherman trying spinner bait. Trails so straight we could see for a mile if the woods wouldn't crowd us so.

That's what *The Palmetto Trail Lowcountry Guide* is all about. Because if - as a local supposed - the height of Lowcountry outdoor recreation once involved a deer stand and boat ramp, that's just not so anymore. Backpacking, trail running and mountain biking are slowly, surely elbowing their way alongside the region's traditional outdoor pursuits. The Palmetto Trail is just a means to that end.

Conceived in 1994 and slated for completion in the early 21st century, the 425-mile Mountains-to-the-Sea Palmetto Trail will eventually meander from a sliver of the Blue Ridge Mountains in South Carolina's northwest corner to the Atlantic Ocean. Along the way, it will connect the state's people, places and cultures by running through 14 different counties. The trail will unite hidden treasures with landmarks, urban streets with wilderness, mountains with sea and everything in between. It is as complex as South Carolina itself.

Nowhere is this canvas laid barer than in the Coastal Plain, the first complete "third" of what will also include Midlands and Upstate portions. Inside, look for descriptions of eight "passages" on the Palmetto Trail within the Coastal Plain:

• **The Awendaw Passage** (7 miles) is the eastern terminus of the Palmetto Trail. The trailhead is located at Buck Hall Recreation Area on the Intracoastal Waterway. Located within a maritime forest the trail follows Awendaw Creek offering sweeping vistas of the Intracoastal Waterway.

• **The Swamp Fox Passage**, runs 47 miles from a trailhead near Awendaw on US 17, through Francis Marion National Forest and on to the Canal Recreation Area trailhead off US 52 outside of Moncks Corner.

• **The Lake Moultrie Passage** runs 24 miles from the Canal Recreation Area trailhead around Lake Moultrie to the Diversion Canal between Lakes Moultrie and Marion.

• **The Eutaw Springs Passage** (20 miles) Leaves the Diversion Canal, traverses some rural dirt roads, an old dairy farm, past the famous Eutaw Springs Battlefield and into the town of Eutawville (pronounced U-taw-ville).

• **The Santee Passage** runs 13 miles from Eutawville to the popular tourist town of Santee. Santee, SC has been designated as the "Gateway to the Lowcountry on the Palmetto Trail."

• **The Lake Marion Passage** runs 33 miles from Santee along the north side of Lake Marion to Mill Creek County Park. It contains some of the most wild and remote areas along the Palmetto Trail.

• **High Hills of the Santee Passage,** a 9-mile section, named for its numerous sandy ridges, connects Mill Creek with Poinsett State Park. In passing through Manchester State Forest the user can sense the history of past Indian trails, early settlers and Revolutionary War soldiers.

• **The Wateree Passage** runs 7 miles from Poinsett Park to the Wateree River to carry the trail user through a tremendous variety of topography, landscapes, plants, and wild animals, all steeped in history. The Wateree floodplain is a real treasure in South Carolina.

If you number among the more provincial outdoor sorts who normally travel to the mountains for adventures, the Coastal Plain portion of the Palmetto Trail is a Cinderella story in waiting. Through 150 plus miles, the trail delves deep into South Carolina life - warts and all. You're going to re-discover the deep, dark swamps of Francis Marion National Forest, the gently rolling hills of the Manchester State Forest and the earthen dike system along Lake Moultrie. Savor the scent of

mosquito repellant as well as a down-home seafood dish. Snuggle up in a seaside bed and breakfast or pitch a tent in a crowded lakeside campground. In other words, accept the Coastal Plain for what it is - an under appreciated wild place and a refuge from our own busy lives.

We've included here everything you'll need to enjoy this section of the Palmetto Trail: detailed trail information and new updated maps. We also provide recommendations about gear, campsites, local eateries, and re-supply points.

Of course, exploring South Carolina's Coastal Plain is not for everyone. The scrubby fields and gloomy swamps are places of understated beauty. Biting insects wake well before dawn and it seems you're never quite far enough from a road, old plantation or factory. Still, the Coastal Plain compels with its own particular aura, drawing visitors time and again, offering its own special rewards.

We can promise that hiking or mountain biking in the Coastal Plain is every bit as challenging as many Sierra Nevada trails. Some of the dirt roads bake like convection ovens; wetland trails can leave your boots waterlogged and stinking. But if you never thought pine forests or swamps could make for a fascinating adventure, just flip through this guide… rediscovery is the purpose of the Palmetto Trail.

How to Use This Guide

This second edition of The Palmetto Trail Lowcountry Guide is unique- both a travel handbook and a hiking companion. Its spiral binding makes it trail friendly and its size is easy enough to fit in a backpack or daypack.

The first part of the book is a history lesson on the Lowcountry and also gives information about the land, the flora and fauna native to this area. Throughout the guide you'll also find lots of anecdotal information about the Lowcountry from folk stories to "locals only" type recommendations on where to eat or stay.

The second part of the book is the official trail guide with detailed descriptions of each of the eight passages in the Lowcountry from the Atlantic Ocean to the Wateree River. At the beginning of each passage is a fold out, detailed trail map that incorporates USGS topographic information. Each map contains UTM grids which represent one square kilometer per grid.

The Palmetto Trail is a young trail and will change in many ways over the next few years. Re-routing, working with private landowners and negotiating with agencies are all part of this Mountains-to-the-Sea trailblazing process. Route changes resulting from maintenance work and relocations are constantly taking place so hikers, mountain bikers and all trail users should be prepared for these eventualities. Therefore, no published route in this guide - no matter how "official" - should be regarded as precisely accurate. We make note of areas that are undergoing

Many sections of the Palmetto Trail border private property. It is imperative that trail-users stay on the trail in these areas.

maintenance, relocations or even across areas of private property. However, none of the information in this guide is a substitute for common sense. We recommend making sure that you familiarize yourself with the trail and surrounding area. It's a good idea to check our website for updates at: www. palmettoconservation.org.

Also, please note that our trail descriptions run from east to west (in effect, inland from the sea). Currently, this is the most common means of exploring the Palmetto Trail. In subsequent editions, look for precise trail descriptions from both directions.

Safety First

It is the responsibility of trail users to plan outings on the Palmetto Trail.

We recommend studying local maps, topographic maps and, in some cases, city maps. You should have water sources and campsites marked and stay acutely aware of your surroundings.

In many cases, the Palmetto Trail follows rural dirt roads through residential neighborhoods. Many of these people are not aware of the Palmetto Trail and may be surprised to see hikers or mountain bikers in their neighborhoods. Be friendly, but remain vigilant about potential conflicts. Similarly, dogs may pose the greatest threat in the Lowcountry since many people allow hounds to run freely. On every trip on the Palmetto Trail we have taken, we have encountered dogs. Most were friendly; a few weren't. The dogs are usually more unnerved by mountain bikers than hikers, but you will want to be prepared for this contingency.

Some of the campsites along the Palmetto Trail allow relaxing lakeside camping.

General Information

What is the Palmetto Trail?

Once completed, the Palmetto Trail will be a 425-mile non-motorized recreational trail traversing the state of South Carolina. The trail begins at Oconee State Park in the Upstate and ends on the coast. Volunteers and employees are building the trail in a series of "passages." Each passage is designed to stand alone and will be accessible for single day or multi-day trips. Together or separate, the passages demonstrate the history, culture and geography of the Palmetto State.

Just as important as the trail itself, the Palmetto Trail will also eventually form a spine for a network of trails in South Carolina — the genesis of a statewide trails system. The planned trail corridor includes the counties of Oconee, Pickens, Greenville, Spartanburg, Union, Laurens, Newberry, Fairfield, Richland, Sumter, Clarendon, Orangeburg, Berkeley and Charleston.

What is Palmetto Conservation?

Palmetto Conservation is a non-profit organization whose mission is to conserve South Carolina's natural and cultural resources, preserve historic buildings and landmarks, and promote outdoor recreation with trails and greenways. The Palmetto Conservation board has adopted five programs to carry out its mission:

• **Conservation of natural and cultural resources**

• **Developing trail and outdoor leadership skills**

• **Promoting public access to natural and historic resources**

• **Military Heritage Preservation**

• **Publishing educational and recreational guides**

The development of the 425-mile Palmetto Trail is one of Palmetto Conservation's signature works.

How can I become a PCF member?

Choose the appropriate category and pay online at the E-store or mail a check to:

Palmetto Conservation Foundation
1314 Lincoln St., Suite 305
Columbia, SC 29201
(803) 771-0870
www.palmettoconservation.org

By becoming a member of Palmetto Conservation Foundation at any level, you will receive a yearly subscription to the Palmetto Explorer newsletter, monthly e-newsletter, annual report, volunteer opportunities including participation in PCF on-the-ground and on-going projects, and a 15% discount on all PCF book or merchandise phone orders.

Membership Levels

General Membership:

___ Individual $35
___ Family $50
___ Friend $100
___ Sponsor $250
___ Benefactor $500

Individual Society & Corporate Memberships:

___ Palmetto Society $1,000
___ Heritage Society $2,500
___ Restoration Society $5,000
___ Millennium Legacy Society $10,000+

Volunteering

Palmetto Conservation is looking for volunteers to help build and maintain trails across South Carolina. Palmetto Conservation sponsors workdays to help train volunteers in ecologically-sound trail building skills.

A dedicated, well-trained corp of volunteers is vital to the completion and maintenance of the trail. We urge all members and anyone interested in learning new skills, working hard, meeting new people and having a good time to add their name to the growing list of Palmetto Trail Volunteers.

Take a few minutes to fill out the information below and send it in today!

Lowcountry coordinator Oliver Buckles (in rear) poses with a crew that helped build a portion of the Swamp Fox Passage.

Please copy this page and mail it to:

Palmetto Conservation
1314 Lincoln Street, Suite 305 • Columbia, SC 29201-3154

Or, email: info@palmettoconservation.org

Name —————————————————————————————

Address ————————————————————————————

City/State ————————————————————— Zip —————

Phone # ————————— Email ———————————————

Special Skills ————————————————————————————

Areas you would like to work ——————————————————————

Trail Marking & Relocation

The Palmetto Trail is marked for travel in both directions (east-to-west and west-to-east). The standard trail blazes are yellow, although the Swamp Fox was built and originally blazed white in 1968. These white blazes remain on the Swamp Fox Passage of the Palmetto Trail. The Eutaw Springs spur trail is also blazed with white paint. On the Manchester State Forest trail, the paint blazes are orange.

Trail blazes are essentially an upside-down exclamation mark; one long blaze below one square-shaped. The entire blaze is about six inches high and two inches wide. Occasionally, in open, treeless areas or at intersections and road crossings, brown, fiberglass posts with white arrows mark directional changes. In some areas where the trail is unmistakable — notably the dike system around Lake Moultrie — there are longer distances between trail markers. Additionally, yellow diamonds are sometimes used to reassure hikers and mountain bikers that they are on the trail.

When the route is not so obvious — for instance, on the spur trails of the Eutaw Springs Passage or in some sections of the Santee Passage — normal marking procedure is to position blazes so that anyone standing at one blaze will always be able to see the next. If you have gone more than a quarter-mile without seeing a blaze, retrace your steps until you locate one and then check to ensure you did not miss a turn. In some residential areas, you must watch for the brown fiberglass posts

This spur trail on the Eutaw Springs Passage is only open from March 2 through September 30, but it's well worth the visit.

near stop signs and street signs.

It's important to note that the Palmetto Trail has changed routes many times in the last several years and will do so many more times in the future. Always follow the marked trail! If it differs from the guidebook description, assume the trail has been recently relocated.

Important Contacts

Hikers, mountain bikers and equestrians using the Palmetto Trail are always encouraged to contact Palmetto Conservation before their trip for advice or notices about trail maintenance and relocations:

Palmetto Conservation
1314 Lincoln St., Suite 305
Columbia, SC 29201
(803) 771-0870
www.palmettoconservation.org

The State Trails Program is working to foster a statewide network of trails and greenways by promoting trail use, management and development. Contact the State Trails Program at:

South Carolina
State Trails Program
1205 Pendleton St.
Columbia, SC 29201
(803) 734-0173
www.SCTrails.net

The Manchester State Forest offers a diverse system of recreational trails on its 25,000 acres.

Manchester State Forest
7640 Headquarters Road
Wedgefield, SC 29168
(803) 494-8196
www.state.sc.us/forest

The USDA Forest Service manages the Francis Marion National Forest and many of the nearby camping and recreation areas in the Lowcountry. For additional information contact either Santee Cooper or the Sewee Visitor Center listed below:

Supervisor:
Forestry & Undeveloped Lands
- Santee Cooper
One Riverwood Drive
Moncks Corner, SC 29461
(843) 761-8000

Witherbee Ranger District
2421 Witherbee Rd.
Cordesville, SC 29434
(843) 336-3248
(843) 336-4789 fax

Sewee Visitor & Environmental
Education Center
5821 Hwy. 17 North
Awendaw, SC 29429
(843) 928-3368
(843) 928-3828 fax
www.fws.gov/seweecenter

The Santee National Wildlife Refuge is managed for migratory waterfowl and offers hiking trails and an auto tour road.

Santee National Wildlife Refuge
2125 Ft. Watson Road
Summerton, SC 29148
(803) 478-2217
www.fws.gov/santee

Before You Go

If you haven't spent much time outdoors in the Coastal Plain, the advice you're about to read will come in very handy. That's because plunging into the Francis Marion National Forest, or along the north side of Lake Marion, is a little different than strolling along the Battery in downtown Charleston or a Kiawah Island beach. Nothing against either activity, mind you. They're great fun… just not helpful preparation for this kind of Coastal Plain adventure.

For the most part, exploring the Palmetto Trail requires very little in the way of special equipment or detailed preparation. The logistics are usually easy: Plan to hike from Point A to Point B, arrange carpooling, grab your gear and hit the trail. Simple enough. But if, say, you don't know what you may encounter en route to Point B or you forget some key bits and pieces, it could become a long trip.

In many ways, exploring the wilderness areas of the Coastal Plain of South Carolina recalls the Southwest desert. From an air-conditioned car, it doesn't look so bad: Flat, open, sunny, not too many obstacles. Then the epic begins. Insects hone in; water runs low; the trailhead seems just a mile further away at each check. In other words, just because there's a fish camp right off the trail doesn't mean you can afford to slack off in preparation.

Outdoor Hazards

In the Coastal Plain, frankly, most of the foreseeable hazards are heat or bug related. Unless you're hiking in a relatively short window from December to February, plan for it to be hot, humid and buggy. But we can't predict all your problems. In truth, your level of preparation should depend on a number of factors that only partially includes weather or insects. A short springtime stroll along the Lake Moultrie dike system will obviously require less foresight than a weekend trip on the Lake Marion Passage.

We can, however, point out eight of the most common hazards:

1. Heat exhaustion and/or hypothermia
2. People & dogs
3. Irritant plants
4. Insects
5. Snakes & alligators
6. Hunting
7. Getting lost
8. Unpurified water

Heat exhaustion and/or hypothermia - If you create more heat than your body can use, it can lead to heat exhaustion and (even worse) heat stroke. This is a very real problem in the Coastal Plain where summer daytime temperatures regularly hover in the 90s and high humidity makes it feel much hotter. If you think somebody is suffering from heat exhaustion or stroke, symptoms include altered mental states, flushed skin, headaches or a rapid pulse. Conversely, it can and does get cold in the Coastal Plain. Coupled with winter precipitation, that can cause serious problems for backcountry hikers. Symptoms of hypothermia include shivering and disorientation.

People & dogs - Some portions of the Palmetto Trail include rural dirt roads and occasional highway crossings. The unfortunate consequence means you might encounter somebody's unleashed dog or poor drivers. It's a good idea to keep an eye on your surroundings and make sure not to put yourself in a compromising situation (e.g., getting into a car with a stranger loitering around a parking area). Many a trail user has admitted feeling safer in the woods than at a trailhead.

Good drinking water is an essential while hiking or biking in the Coastal Plain. Even with water available at a number of locations on the trail, users need to plan ahead.

Irritant plants - Needless to say, poison ivy, oak and sumac cause an inordinate amount of grief when you consider that it's not hard to identify and avoid them. Poison ivy and oak come in leaves grouped in clusters of threes. In the Southeast, poison sumac also poses a problem because it can grow in swamps and river bottoms. Although related to poison ivy and oak, it actually grows as a small tree with pale-gray bark and leaves divided into seven or 11 leaflets.

Insects - The mosquitoes in and around Atlantic Coastal Plain and Santee Cooper country are, in a word, legendary. In Colonial times, malaria wiped out entire settlements and the leisure classes regularly escaped mosquito-prone areas by heading north. So just go on and accept it: You will emerge from this trip with mosquito bites. Unfortunately, that may not be all, either. Gnats, deerflies, wasps, ticks, fire ants and chiggers can make your trailside life quite difficult. That said,

insect repellant should be required for any backcountry trip on the Palmetto Trail. Also make sure to examine yourself every night for ticks - no matter the time of year.

Snakes and alligators - There are six species of poisonous snakes in South Carolina. But the vast majority of snakes you'll see along the Palmetto Trail are harmless. Among the more common are the black and white Eastern king snake and (primarily black) rat snake. However, the Atlantic Coastal Plain provides an excellent home for poisonous snakes such as the copperhead, cottonmouth and canebrake rattlesnake. They most commonly inhabit debris piles, stumps and brush far from most human activity, though. Avoiding them is usually simple enough: Just give the snake a wide berth. Alligators, meanwhile, are the largest land carnivores in the state and you'll usually find them in fresh or mildly brackish water — if you're lucky. We say this because these wily creatures don't usually draw much attention to themselves. Still, you should not swim in water inhabited by large alligators and remember to keep pets leashed since alligators occasionally confuse dogs for their normal diet of small mammals, fish and other reptiles. Interestingly, of the roughly 750 alligator complaints investigated by the S.C. Dept. of Natural Resources (DNR) each year, more than half involve alligators less than five feet long. These alligators' largest meals are usually turtles. According to DNR, in the last 25 years there have been seven alligator attacks in S.C, and half of those were provoked. None were fatal. Consider yourself enlightened.

Hunting - Call yourself an "outdoorsman" in South Carolina and it usually means one of three things: You hunt, fish or do some combination of the two. Fishing doesn't pose much of a problem to hikers. However, it's no fun to stumble out of the brush within sight of a deer stand early on a fall weekend morning. Although hunters and hikers coexist rather well, you should consider checking with land managers before venturing onto the trail. Wear bright clothing during hunting seasons, travel in groups and make noise. If you're still unsure about hunting seasons, contact the Dept. of Natural Resources at (800) 734-3886.

Getting lost - Stay on designated trails. Every time you tread in an area that was previously untouched, you are altering the terrain for subsequent generations… and you also risk losing the trail. If you do get lost, don't panic and try to backtrack by looking for familiar landmarks. The best way to avoid getting lost is to carry a topographic map and a compass. You can purchase USGS topos in many outdoor outfitter shops or contact SC Mapping Services, 5 Geology Road, Columbia, SC, 29210, (803) 896-7338 or www.scgs.state.sc.us

Unpurified water - Unless it's polluted, drinking unpurified water won't usually

Occasional hand pumps allow trail-users to resupply with potable water while in the backcountry.

catch up with you until after you're home from a trip. But it will catch up with you eventually and you won't like it when it does. Regardless of how pristine a natural water source may look, it's a good bet that it carries microorganisms such as giardia or cryptosporidium. These illnesses can take from two to 20 days to manifest and will make you extremely uncomfortable while they run their course. Consider boiling, filtering or treating water with iodine unless you're absolutely sure it's potable.

Planning

Whether you're hiking, mountain biking or horseback riding along the Palmetto Trail, you'll need to carry some essentials on the trip. This may sound silly — especially in a populated area like the Coastal Plain — but you are on your own out there and you should approach every trip as such.

If you want to get down to the basics, backcountry travel doesn't require much specialized knowledge. Sometimes all you need is a good sense of direction. But in today's society, when people are more likely to do their exploring by watching the Outdoor Life Network, a little helpful preparation will pay off in the long run. Some trip essentials include:

1. Trail or topographic map
2. Compass
3. Adequate water and food
4. Adequate clothing (this includes rain gear and/or sunglasses)
5. Knife
6. First-aid kit
7. Headlamp or flashlight
8. Waterproof matches
9. Signaling device (Whistle, mirror)
10. Insect repellant

Anne Close hiking during a cold day on the Swamp Fox Passage

In lieu of a comprehensive section on first-aid, you might want to consider taking a Wilderness First Responder course through Wilderness Medical Associates or some basic Red Cross first-aid techniques. Additionally, some books do an excellent job of covering the matter:

• Isaac, Jeff and Peter Goth, *The Outward Bound Wilderness First-Aid Handbook,* New York: Wilderness Medical Associates, 1997.

• Preston, Gilbert, *Wilderness First Aid: When You Can't Call 911,* Helena: Falcon Press, 1998.

• Weiss, Eric A. *Wilderness 911: A Step-by-Step Guide for Medical Emergencies and Improvised Care in the Backcountry,* Seattle: The Mountaineers, 1997.

Mountain Biking

Other — perhaps more specialized — equipment will depend on the means you decide to travel on the Palmetto Trail. For instance, mountain biking essentials would include all of the previously mentioned gear plus a few additional ones:

1. Tool kit - This should include your spare pump, tube and a patch kit. (Free hint!

Make sure you can change your tires at home before you hit the trail.) A mini-kit for longer trips might include adjustable wrench, screwdriver, Allen wrenches and a chain tool.

2. Helmet

International Mountain Bike Association (IMBA) Rules of the Trail

• Ride on open trails only: Respect trail and road closures, avoid trespassing on private lands, obtain permits and permission where required. Federal and state wilderness areas are closed to cycling. The way you ride will influence subsequent trail management and decisions.

• Leave no trace: Be sensitive to the trail beneath you. Avoid riding immediately after heavy rain or when the trail surface is soft and muddy (in the Lowcountry that doesn't always apply since the trail is often soft and muddy). Practice low-impact cycling. This means staying on existing trails and not creating new ones. Pack out everything you pack in and hopefully some trash left by another, less-considerate trail user.

Much of the Palmetto Trail is ideally suited for mountain bikes with some long, straight sections and challenging dips and turns, along with some wet conditions thrown in for good measure.

- Control your bicycle: Obey all bicycle speed regulations and recommendations.

- Always yield the trail: Multiple use trail guidelines stipulate that mountain bikers yield to hikers and equestrians. A friendly greeting works well and you can also show respect by slowing to a walking pace or even stopping, particularly when you encounter horses.

- Never scare animals: You will startle all animals by unannounced approach, sudden movements or loud noises. This can be dangerous for you, other trail users and the animals themselves. Use extra care when passing horses and follow directions from equestrians if you're uncertain.

- Plan ahead: Know your limitations, your equipment and the area in which you plan to ride. You must approach mountain biking with a self-sufficient mindset. Keep your equipment in good shape and carry necessary supplies for changing weather or other conditions.

Horseback Riding

The fragile, often wet condition of the Palmetto Trail in the Coastal Plain means that land managers do not allow equestrians here. The exceptions are a six-mile portion of the Swamp Fox Passage that overlaps with the Jericho Horse Trail and the 7 miles through Manchester State Forest in the High Hills Passage. *Please heed this rule.*

There are other horseback-riding opportunities in the region, however. The S.C. Horsemen's Council has taken great pains to promote trail etiquette and trail safety tips. While trail riding, it's an equestrian's duty to know the trail and use common courtesy.

These guidelines are from the S.C. Horsemen's Council:

- Know the local rules. Courtesy is the best safety on the trail. Know where you're permitted to ride and where you're not. Respect private property and closed areas.

- Minimize impact by staying on designated trails and avoiding muddy conditions. Don't cut switchbacks or take shortcuts; it sends a poor message about our sport.

- Always be courteous when you pass other trail users. Say hello. Tell people how many are in your party. Pass with care and if you're uncertain whether you can pass, just ask.

- Always speak in a calm voice when approaching horses. A horse's vision is restricted, but its hearing is acute. The horse needs to recognize you as a human. Avoid any sudden movements.

- Leave gates as you find them. Obey gate closures and regulatory signs.

- Know your horse's limitations.

- Ride at a controlled speed. Be especially careful when visibility is impaired.

- Let other trail riders know when it is safe to pass your horse.

- A hand out and down is a warning for others to slow down or stop.

- Keep the trailhead and trail clear of manure and trash.

- At trailside rest stops, even short ones, tie off your horse. This prevents horses from damaging trees or vegetation and is courteous to other trail users by helping reduce wear and tear on the trail. Before you move on, scatter the manure.

Weather Considerations

If you always thought about traveling to the Coastal Plain in the summer so you could frolic on the beaches, well, that's still a good plan. But that isn't necessarily the best time to explore the Palmetto Trail. According to Southeast Regional Climate Center records (from 1971 to 2000), the average July high temperature at the Pinopolis Dam is 91.6 degrees. The average precipitation is 5.63 inches. So what's the forecast? Hot and humid... almost year-round.

While you can usually find a nice offshore breeze on the beach, the wind doesn't usually make it far enough inland to cool off the trails. Unless you've built up a tolerance to the heat and humidity of a South Carolina summer, best to avoid the Palmetto Trail during this time of year.

Similarly, visitors don't always realize that the Lowcountry gets most of its rainfall in the summer months, far more than from November through March (another strike against summertime exploring). Convectional rain occurs often on humid summer days. April, incidentally, is one of the driest months in the region, which makes it a great time to do some outdoor exploring. A relatively slim chance of snow or other frozen precipitation (Charleston, for instance, averages 0.1 inch of snow from January through March) also makes winters a great time for invigorating pursuits such as hiking and mountain biking. Spend enough time out there and you will eventually encounter freezing rain, though, so best be prepared for some cold weather conditions.

Southeast Regional Climate Center:
Weather and Climate Readings at Pinopolis Dam (near Moncks Corner)

Month	Lo Temp.	Hi Temp.	Avg. Temp.	Avg. Prcp.
Jan.	35.1	56.7	45.9	4.22
Feb.	37.1	60.5	48.8	3.56
March	43.6	67.9	55.8	3.88
April	50.3	75.6	63.0	3.19
May	58.6	82.7	70.7	4.13
June	66.1	88.4	79.1	5.51
July	70.2	91.6	80.9	5.63
Aug.	69.4	89.8	79.6	6.59
Sept.	64.1	85.3	74.7	4.63
Oct.	53.1	76.6	64.9	3.09
Nov.	43.1	66.6	54.7	2.63
Dec.	38.2	60.6	49.4	3.69

A Brief History of the Lowcountry

Before European Exploration

In the 16th century, when Spanish conquistadors first set foot in the land we would eventually call South Carolina, a vast frontier of swamps and dense woodlands lay before them. Though wild and filled with unfamiliar creatures, it wasn't entirely unoccupied. Some ethnologists believe people had been living there for 16,000 years — perhaps since the Ice Age. South Carolina's Lowcountry has been shaped by eons of human drama, fortitude and fate.

When migrating tribes with crude tool making and hunting skills pushed into South Carolina during the Ice Age, they might have been following huge game such as mammoth and mastodon. These creatures would have provided everything the people of the Pleistocene era needed for sustenance until the Ice Age finally ended and the region underwent a major weather-induced hangover. And so the early Indians adapted as best they could; some migrated to the Coastal Plain where they established civilizations fed by shellfish, small mammals, fish and fowl. A number of modern-day historic sites in the Lowcountry observe the achievements of these people; the Sewee Shell Mound, for instance, is a 4,000 year-old archaeological site not far from the Awendaw trailhead of the Swamp Fox Passage. The ring of oyster shells marks nothing more than an ancient trash heap. But it also offers a window into life on the Coast with the region's early settlers.

Early Explorers

A number of Indian settlements sprung up in South Carolina before Europeans arrived, most notably the city of Cofitachequi in today's Kershaw County on the Wateree River. Some estimates place the "state's" Indian population at roughly 15,000 by the mid 16th century. Of all these peoples, the Coastal Indians may have enjoyed the easiest life. They broke up into small but numerous tribes who fanned out over the region to prosper peacefully. Today, their European-given names — Wando, Edisto, Sewee, Etiwan and Combahee — pepper the Coastal Plain.

None of them, however, could have been prepared for the marauding Spanish explorers of the 16th century. Fortunately, the Indians didn't have to do much to stave off the early explorers. The few reconnaissance missions that pushed into the Coastal Plain perished rather quickly due to a combination of mutiny, starvation, or mosquito-born malaria. The land — especially then — was unforgiving. Indigenous peoples saw no other visitors for nearly four generations, but that didn't mean the land-hungry Europeans had forgotten about the new world's promise.

By the middle of the 17th century and with Spain on the decline, the English began making various claims to a land they first called "Carolana" and later, "Carolina." In 1663, the newly restored King Charles II appointed eight noblemen as "lords proprietors" of the region. We don't need to know all of these men, but should note some important landmarks named for Anthony Ashley-Cooper, Sir William Berkeley and counselor George Monck. Still, the settlement of Carolina was excruciatingly slow and, despite lavish spending on exploration, the original lords saw no return from their new holdings. It would be more than seven years before the first permanent English settlement in Carolina would succeed.

A Colony Takes Root

After several failures in Florida,

the English in 1670 finally managed to establish residence beside two rivers, the Ashley and Cooper. They named their settlement Charles Town — for their king, naturally — and quickly set about establishing fortifications, trading routes and plowing fields. Just 30 years later, the colony had grown into the crown jewel of England's new world colonies. Despite a little trouble from the Spanish and their sympathetic Indian acquaintances, the English enjoyed relatively few such difficulties. Native-born people, of course, had been living nearby already: Eutaw, Sewee, Wando and Santee Indians all lived in the Lowcountry well before colonists arrived. But a combination of smallpox and other European diseases decimated their ranks well before the Revolutionary War, leaving white men largely free to spread throughout the region in search of cheaper land and better livelihoods.

The early settlers of South Carolina — like their descendents — showed extraordinary resilience in the face of challenge. Through attacks from pirates, prolonged Indian battles, such as the

Lowcountry settlers spread out across the fertile land to farm for indigo and cotton. This old cabin is at Kensington Field.

Yemassee War, and colonial infighting, Carolina continued to prosper. By the early 18th century, rice had become the primary cash crop for Lowcountry residents because it thrived in the region's vast wetlands. An entire culture soon grew around its production, allowing the aristocratic planters to amass wealth, political power and thousands of acres of land. However, rice also necessitated a huge demand for laborers and South Carolina quickly became the mainland's largest slave importer. The trade extended beyond people, though.

For several decades, Charles Town almost resembled a Western frontier town. Fur and deerskin traders brought pack trains straight into the city, fresh from dealing with Creeks, Choctaws, Cherokee or Catawba Indians. An Indian trader named George Sterling pushed into the area around present-day Orangeburg in 1704, which earned its name for William, Prince of Orange and son-in-law of King George II of England. The city's booming economy allowed its residents and landowners to spread north, west and south, opening new rice fields and plantations as they went.

In their wake, the planters also left a legacy of canal-fed swamps separated by elaborate dike systems. Some of the Palmetto Trail — notably sections of the Swamp Fox Passage around Wadboo Swamp — crisscrosses swampland by using these ancient dikes. Ironically, the trails still allow access to places normally inhabited only by alligators and towering bald cypress trees.

But dependence on a single cash crop eventually hurt the colony as European demand for rice shrank. Farmers eventually began experimenting with another crop: indigo. By the mid 1700s, a combination of rice, forest products and indigo had brought prosperity to

Lowcountry landowners. To encourage settlement beyond Charleston, the General Assembly began granting townships. In 1735, a colony of several hundred Swiss, German and Dutch immigrants formed a community on the fertile banks of the North Edisto River. Orangeburg soon became well established and successful; the river provided transportation to the port of Charleston for additional agricultural products and a public road connected the cities by 1737.

Things might have remained relatively peaceful had England not bumbled its way into a revolution.

American Revolution:
From Reluctance to Rebellion in the Lowcountry

Although the origins of the Revolutionary War are too numerous to detail here, suffice it to say that in the decade before 1776 there was considerable controversy among Lowcountry colonists about whether they should remain loyal to the throne. But when blood began spilling in New England — and even closer to home at the town of Ninety Six — Lowcountry residents soon joined the remainder of the rebellious Colonists. In 1776, as the debate over independence continued in Philadelphia, the British made an early play for Charleston and attacked by sea. The bombardment failed and the Lowcountry saw no significant action for nearly four years. The next time, humbled by their previous failure, the English overwhelmed Charleston by land. Convinced the port city was the strategic key to the South, the British also erringly persuaded themselves the territory would remain safe for the rest of the war. History, of course, proved them wrong, since the Lowcountry proved a hugely important bastion of opposition.

South Carolina produced its share of Revolutionary heroes, but none would earn such lasting repute in the Lowcountry as Gen. Francis Marion. From various strongholds in the swamps of Berkeley County and elsewhere in the Pee Dee, the wily general led an extraordinary resistance campaign against the British. His admirers christened him "Swamp Fox" for his unusual tactics: Marion emerged from the inaccessible wetlands only so he might engage British forces in sporadic guerilla warfare. The general had his first taste of battle while manning cannons on Sullivan's Island. But after the British besieged Charleston, Marion and a troop of hard-riding rebels retreated to the swamps where they remained for the rest of the war. Marion kept the British supply lines in constant disruption and eventually overwhelmed several British outposts. Today, his gravesite sits at the end of a shady driveway off SC 45 on the shores of Lake Moultrie and receives far less attention than it should.

By mid-1781, the tide had turned elsewhere in South Carolina and the only remaining British force of any size lay north of Charleston at Eutaw Springs. The Americans finally struck on Sept. 8, 1781 and what ensued is remembered as one of the hardest fought battles of the war. Both sides claimed victory in what could best be characterized as a draw, but the British realized they would have to fall back to Charleston. Just over a year later — in December 1782 — the last British evacuated the port city and conceded victory. Skirmishes continued across the Upstate frontier for years afterward, but the Lowcountry fairly soon settled into a peaceful existence.

A False Hope: Cotton and the Road to War

Ironically, although the Colonists managed to shed their British albatross, the Lowcountry would never again recapture its previous prosperity. In the years between the Revolutionary War and the Civil War, South Carolina produced a throng of brilliant men, and residents of the Upstate and Lowcountry began working together to ensure a prosperous economy. But at the same time, South Carolina began trudging down a road to ruin. Reliance on the one-crop system of cotton helped spread slavery throughout the state, discouraged interest

D E T O U R S

Tar pits & Moonshine

In pre-Revolutionary War times, one of the most important industries in Berkeley County was the production of tar and pitch for ship construction and maintenance. In several places along the Swamp Fox Trail — if you know where to look — you can still see mounds where colonial workers extracted pitch from pine trees. The trail even passes right over one near Harleston Dam Swamp.

By the 20th century, Berkeley County was earning a different reputation: Moonshine hub. During prohibition, bootleggers would hide in the region's vast swamps where they produced enough "liquid corn" to supply armies of deprived drinkers. Because it was so cheap, local bootleggers continued to make moonshine well after prohibition.

in manufacturing, produced an agrarian society disinterested in public education and ultimately divided the entire nation.

One could hardly blame the Lowcountry planters at first. Faced with finding new cash crops after their markets in Europe dried up, the invention of the cotton gin in 1793 initially seemed a salvation. Similarly, cotton had to be transported to the important port city of Charleston, so those who weren't actually growing the crop stayed busy by constructing canals or roadways. But the state's fertile land couldn't provide forever and the state's economy began to weaken. For the next 70 years — until men actually took up arms against each other — there existed an uneasy peace between the landed aristocracy of the South and the Northern industrialists. The drama unfolded in excruciating fashion: levies on European exports and imports penalized Southern traders for not dealing with the North; the abolitionist movement and political fallout from the Mexican War further isolated Southern landowners. And so, in1861, the first shots of the Civil War rang out in Charleston's Harbor.

War and a Difficult Reconstruction

Despite South Carolina's important contribution to starting the Civil War (and aside from the Union's long crusade to take Charleston) the state escaped much bloodshed on its own soil until 1865. In that year, Gen. William T. Sherman marched from Savannah through Columbia, allowing his Union troops to devastate a swath some 60 miles wide and leave much of the state in ruin. But while South Carolina escaped most major battles, its population suffered terribly: Historians suggest nearly a quarter of South Carolina's fighting age male population died in the war. In the Lowcountry especially (where plantations required manpower and a large workforce) the post-war years meant terrible poverty and an exceedingly painful reconstruction. The Emancipation Proclamation freed South Carolina slaves — the very workers who constituted Lowcountry planters' primary capital investments. So with no workforce and no money to hire new recruits, the landowners could not grow their crops. Some timber barons turned to wide-scale lumbering and began clearing huge parcels of land for timber interests.

The initial years of Reconstruction are among the darkest times in South Carolina's history. For most of the first decade after the Civil War, federal troops

DETOURS

Battle of Eutaw Springs

On Sept. 8, 1781, American and British troops engaged in the last significant battle of the Revolutionary War fought on South Carolina soil: the Battle of Eutaw Springs. The battle involved sizeable forces of over 1,000 on each side and was several weeks in coming. By August of 1781 — as American troops were winning several key battles in the North — Gen. Nathanael Greene's American army and Col. Alexander Stewart's British forces were cautiously eyeing one another from camps across the Wateree River.

Things might have remained that way for longer until Gen. George Washington suggested Greene resume offensive operations against the British. Washington was planning a major, combined American-French move against the British in Virginia and wanted to prevent British reinforcements from heading his way. So with his orders in hand, Greene broke camp and began looking for a way to cross the Wateree. Meanwhile, Stewart retreated to a strong position around Eutaw Springs.

Greene (with Gen. Francis Marion in command of the militia) attacked

Eutaw Springs Battleground, a small park off SC 6 has several historical markers and graves that commemorate this hugely important battle.

Stewart at dawn, first with rounds from Marion's militia and later in bloody hand-to-hand combat that beat the British back to their encampment. The hungry, naked Continentals stopped to pillage the camp for food and drink, allowing the opposing army to regroup and drive them back. Both sides claimed victory in the battle, and in truth neither won: Americans and British suffered a 30 percent casualty rate.

Fearing a second attack, however, Stewart retreated first to Moncks Corner and later to Charleston where he remained for a year until the British finally evacuated for good.

Legends of the Swamp Fox

No Lowcountry citizen before or since Revolutionary War Gen. Francis Marion has inspired so many myths, half-truths and folk tales. From his hideouts on Snows Island, in the Great White Marsh of the Pee Dee and all along today's Palmetto Trail, the little Huguenot general spent the initial years of the Revolutionary War waging a lonely uprising against the British armies who had so easily overtaken South Carolina.

It was only because of Marion's intuitive grasp of guerilla warfare that the rebels were able to turn the tide. He scraped together a loyal band of troops, mostly men who had been driven from their families by the Tory armies and who were experienced woodsmen, able to survive for days at a time on the land. Among his earliest victories were surprise battles at "Blue Savannah" (an open area on the Little Pee Dee River) and Black Mingo (a creek off the Little Pee Dee.) Here, he employed tactics that would cement his reputation: After riding 30 miles and crossing three rivers during daytime, Marion's determined troops struck under cover of darkness.

The Battle of Black Mingo lasted only 15 minutes, but it was a bloody defeat for the Loyalists. Marion's troops took British guns, ammunition and horses — including a mount that Marion took for his own and renamed Ball (after its former rider, defeated British Col. John Coming Ball!). The dashing 48-year-old Marion treated his Loyalist prisoners with such respect that several renounced the King and joined the patriots.

By 1780 — as Robert D. Bass wrote in his excellent biography, *Swamp Fox* — Marion had become the scourge of the British. He hid in unknown camps, crept stealthily on raids and led enough midnight attacks to bring him to the attention of British high command. Eventually, Lord Cornwallis sent Lt. Col. Banastre Tarleton after Marion, who simply escaped into a bog near Kingstree. Faced with either a futile chase of Marion or turning north to fight Thomas Sumter (the "Gamecock"), Tarleton chose the latter and uttered the famous epithet that would eventually follow Marion everywhere: "Come, my boys!" Tarleton cried in his thick Lancashire accent. "Let us go back and find the Gamecock. But as for this damned old fox, the devil himself could not catch him!"

occupied the state and added to the burden of post-war rebuilding. State government remained in turmoil for decades as whites struggled to accept the newly freed blacks. But South Carolina did recover; by the end of the 19th century, Lowcountry plantations were transporting cotton to the Upstate rather than New England. The textile industry boomed, providing new opportunity. Of course, it couldn't last.

In 1919, the boll weevil devastated the cotton crop and paved the way for a new challenge: the Great Depression.

Digging Out of One Pit By Building Two:

Creation of Santee Cooper leads to Lakes Moultrie and Marion

Although President Franklin D. Roosevelt made the South's recovery a

Francis Marion's tomb sits at the end of a shady driveway off SC 45 between Lakes Moultrie and Marion. The land was once his brother's plantation, Belle Isle.

Marion continued haranguing British troops for the remainder of the war and was on hand at the final significant battle in South Carolina, the Battle of Eutaw Springs. As the war closed, he set up camp at Wadboo and roamed east of the Cooper until the British finally withdrew from Charleston in 1782. Marion returned to find his plantation at Pond Bluff in ruins, but he overcame and served in the S.C.

House. He eventually married in 1786 (his first cousin, Mary Esther) and died at the age of 63 in 1795. He was buried at the family cemetery on Gabriel's Plantation on Belle Isle. You can still read the inscription on his tomb today. It says, in part: "History will record his worth, and rising generations embalm his memory as one of the most distinguished Patriots and Heroes of the American Revolution."

cornerstone of his first administration's economic policy, there was already a movement underfoot to change the Lowcountry way of life. The Depression exacerbated its problems, but there was no denying that — outside Charleston proper — things were already bad in the Lowcountry. Sparsely populated and dependent upon a pre-Civil War way of life, residents of Lowcountry counties

such as Berkeley, Orangeburg, and the isolated reaches of Charleston struggled to keep their heads above water, mainly by sustenance farming.

But Columbia businessman T.C. Williams thought he knew of one way to address their problems. Williams wanted to dam the Santee and Cooper Rivers and build a hydroelectric plant that could supply power to the rural areas of South

Carolina and possibly create a navigable route from Columbia to Charleston. The goal was essentially simple: Divert the Santee River into the Cooper to increase its flow and generate more electricity. It took nearly 14 years of cajoling residents and convincing skeptical scientists. But in 1934, the South Carolina government created a public service authority to tackle the job. What ensued was the largest clearing operation in the nation's history (some 225 square-miles of swampland), removal of 40 million cubic yards of earth to form Lakes Marion and Moultrie, creation of 42 dams and dikes, and construction of a 6.5-mile diversion canal. Santee Cooper country was born.

The immediate consequences were a boom to the depressed region. Huge manufacturing plants and industry began moving to the Coastal Plain, lured by low-cost electricity and a needy workforce. Lakes Marion and Moultrie quickly became popular tourist destinations with reputations for world-class fishing, hunting and boating. The region's economy changed almost overnight.

Still, Santee Cooper hasn't meant all good things. Scientists finally realized that by diverting the Santee's waters into the Cooper, they were also exacerbating the amount of sediment deposited into Charleston Harbor. Building a costly "re-diversion" canal in the 1980s made sure roughly 80 percent of the Santee's water would flow back into the river downstream after doing its job of creating electricity. The Palmetto Trail offers an up-close view of the entire system. The northern trailhead of the Swamp Fox Passage ends at the Canal Recreation Area on the shores of Lake Moultrie. To continue north (on the aptly-named Lake Moultrie Passage), you will wind along the lake for some 24 miles and pass the Rediversion Canal near Russellville, the Old Canal and the Diversion Canal. The Lake Marion Passage crosses Lake Marion on an abandoned road and runs along the north side of the lake passing near Sparkleberry Swamp. Santee Cooper country is a hugely important facet of the Palmetto Trail.

Lowcountry Life at the Millennium

The second half of the 20th century — after creation of Santee Cooper — was an intriguing time for the Coastal Plain. "Nature-based" tourism took hold along the lakes and you can now find a fish camp, guide service or grocery and landing at seemingly every crossroads. Huge new industrial complexes and refineries such as Nucor and Alcoa provide some jobs while the paper and packaging manufacturer Mead Westvaco has continued to develop its vast land holdings and timber interests throughout the Coastal Plain. Chemical and manufacturing companies such as Georgia Pacific compete for workers with companies mining for limestone.

But there remains an extraordinary amount of poverty in the region and the Palmetto Trail winds through some areas that may never emerge from their decades-long depression. That said, by many accounts, Coastal Plain life in the early 21st century is better than ever. In its journey from the shores of the Atlantic Ocean through Francis Marion National Forest, Santee Cooper country and into the Upper Coastal Plain, the Palmetto Trail highlights just a few of the region's bright spots. The trail intentionally dives

Lowcountry Ghosts

South Carolina has a rich folklore, in part because the residents of its Lowcountry so valued oral history and conversation. And while the region has produced some fine authors, many historians say our best folk tales are ghost stories. The coast around Beaufort seemed to produce more stories than anywhere else. But Nancy Rhyne's eerie book, *Tales of the South Carolina Low Country,* also recounts a strange incident from Runnymede Plantation on the south side of Charleston's Magnolia Gardens.

Seems two school-age brothers played a prank on the plantation residents in 1974. During a foray deep into the woods, they came upon an African-American burial ground and noticed some personal possessions had been placed atop the graves. A tradition with deep African roots, the plantation residents believed the practice would keep people from coming back for these things. However, they also believed that if one of these items were removed or tampered with in any way, the dead would impart swift and dreadful retribution.

The brothers, undaunted by such talk, apparently took a drinking glass and brought it back to Charleston. As word spread of the misdeed, the boys returned the object, but it was to no avail. The next day, the plane taking them to school in North Carolina crashed outside Charlotte. Locals remain convinced to this day that it was a reprisal by the spirit of the dead person whose grave had been violated the day before.

Since these burial grounds are found throughout the Lowcountry and may exist not far from the Palmetto Trail, consider yourself warned!

Cemeteries, such as this one near Cordesville, are a common occurrence in the Lowcountry and good fodder for ghost stories.

In part because of new recreational opportunities like the Palmetto Trail, Lowcountry life in the early twenty-first century is better than ever. More and more people are enjoying hiking, camping, biking and equestrian use in the great out-of-doors.

back and forth between populated areas and rural ones offering ample opportunity to experience the region's culture in a series of day-trips or as a through-hike.

Ironically — after years of manipulating the landscape to the whims of agriculture and industry — some Coastal Plain counties are among the state's leaders in preserving what remains of their green space. Perhaps that's because almost two decades ago

Hurricane Hugo devastated the region, particularly Francis Marion National Forest. The forest has been managed primarily for timber interests since its inception in 1936, but today includes nearly 120 miles of recreational trails. The U.S. Forest Service is

DETOURS

Whoppers!
Santee Cooper Fishing

So you think you can tell the difference between a fish tale and fishy ones?

Try these on for size: One Arkansas blue catfish pulled out of these lakes weighed in at 109.4 pounds. Another channel cat came in at 58 pounds.

In fact, both stories are true, evidence of the amazing fishing available on both Lake Marion and Moultrie. A plastic replica of the 109-pound catfish can be seen in the Berkeley Chamber of Commerce office. Anglers from all over have been traveling to these lakes for years because they offer such great habitat for bream, crappie, largemouth bass, stripers, white bass and catfish. Because the land wasn't fully cleared before the floodgates closed, fish can dart back and forth between cypress trees since they offer shelter from birds.

Striped bass, in particular, are at home on these waters. When the dam across the Santee River impounded Lake Moultrie in 1942, biologists observed stripers coming up from the ocean and into the Cooper River to spawn. However, the fish entered Lake Moultrie

The Santee Cooper lake system can produce some big fish but the really big whoppers are often in the stories told after a day of fishing along the Palmetto Trail.

through the Pinopolis Lock and became landlocked. By a quirk of nature, the Santee Cooper lakes and the rivers leading to them were an ideal freshwater habitat for that saltwater fish. Since then, the stripers have been spawning and living year-round in these waters.

slowly awakening to the need for recreational opportunity in its green spaces and nowhere is that more obvious than Francis Marion National Forest. Similarly, Berkeley County has aggressively zoned all of its 1,230 square miles to fight the kind of sprawl that

has plagued other parts of South Carolina. Clarendon and lower Sumter Counties haven't seen the growth like other parts of the Coastal Plain and the trail user will get a feel for the wilder side of South Carolina.

The Land

For hundreds of years — and well before geologists jumped into the game — South Carolinians have divided their state into three broad areas: the Lowcountry, Midlands and Upstate. Within those regions, people also use any number of other terms to describe a particular corner of the state. In the mountains, for instance, locals sometimes refer to the extreme northwest as the Blue Ridge Escarpment and everything to the southeast as the Foothills and Piedmont. The Midlands includes the Savannah River Valley and the Sandhills, while the Lowcountry contains the Pee Dee, Grand Strand, Sea Islands and the Coastal Zone — a narrow strip along the Atlantic Ocean. Another way to divide the state — and probably the most geographically proper — is Coastal Plain, Sandhills, Piedmont and Mountains.

For our purposes, however, this guide will concentrate on what we'll consider the Lowcountry. That includes everything in the Coastal Plain from the shores of the Atlantic through the Francis Marion National Forest and on into the Sandhills. The Lowcountry was the first portion of

South Carolina settled by Europeans and thus contains some of the state's oldest cities and historical sites. The terrain has always been fertile, which led early settlers to spread out over a wide area and harvest much of the land's bounty.

Consequently, there's no true backcountry left in the Coastal Plain. Still, the region's numerous salt marshes, Carolina bays, swamps and wetlands offer a lifetime's worth of temptation.

Forests and Swamps

Some 85 percent of the 250,000-acre Francis Marion National Forest is upland forest, a mixture of loblolly and longleaf pines, oaks and hickories while the Manchester State Forest is gently rolling sand ridges with a mix of pine and hardwood trees. But hundreds of years ago these woods looked very different; a long history of human occupation and exploitation has wrought many changes in the natural environment. In the relatively brief period between human settlement and the 20th century, the forest went from a proud example of longleaf pine ecosystem to an austere landscape decimated by uncontrolled lumbering, clearing for rice plantations and

Some 85 percent of the 250,000-acre Francis Marion National Forest is upland forest.

eventually even Hurricane Hugo (though that was a more "natural" cleansing).

Trees of an upland forest make their homes primarily on sand "ridges" that were once beaches millions of years ago when the ocean was further inland. Longleaf pine need fire to regenerate and grow, so the U.S. Forest Service has taken great pains to help restore the forest by using careful prescribed burns.

Hurricane Hugo

Visit the Coastal Plain often enough and you're bound to hear a local say something to the effect of, "Oh, we had to completely abandon that house after Hugo." That's because the Category 4 hurricane that slammed into the Coastal Plain on Sept. 21, 1989 became the defining weather event for a generation.

As it was bearing down on the region with 135 mph winds and a huge 20-foot storm surge, most Lowcountry citizens fled inland. The storm followed, though, pushing 200 miles into the state and ravaging a corridor from Charleston to Columbia and Charlotte. Although Hugo killed 49 people in the U.S., only 17 died in South Carolina, a toll far less than it could have been. However, the storm did $5 billion in property damage — still among the costliest storms in U.S. history — and almost completely re-shaped the Coastal Plain's natural environment in one night.

Consider Francis Marion National Forest where officials estimate between 70 and 80 percent of the trees snapped during the five-hour storm. The storm's tidal surge, meanwhile, completely washed over barrier islands such as Bull and Capers, leveling entire forests of loblolly pine and oak. You could have visited the Swamp Fox Trail not long after the storm and been among the tallest things in the forest. Human dramas gave the storm added punch. In McClellanville, for instance, 1,200 hardy villagers of nearby fishing

towns thought they could ride out the storm inside then-new Lincoln High School. They did — but just barely. As the full fury of the storm raged overhead, the tidal surge began spilling into the school and seawater rose to a height of six feet. People stood on tables, chairs and removed ceiling panels to avoid the water. Astonishingly, nobody was hurt and the water finally began to recede a few hours before dawn. Of course, nearly every building in the town sustained damage and it took almost five years to rebuild.

The Coastal Plain has made an extraordinary recovery in the two decades since Hugo. Wildlife biologists have restored over 1,000 red-cockaded woodpecker nests in tree cavities throughout the region and guided the recovery of the long-leaf pine population so it can keep pace with the more aggressive loblolly pine. Hugo left a different, but no less resilient, Lowcountry in its wake.

Beyond the Obvious

In addition to upland forest and swamps, the Coastal Plain also includes other important terrain. The Santee Delta, for instance, is a zone along the coast roughly 20 miles wide from Cape Romain National Wildlife Refuge north to Winyah Bay south of Georgetown. It's the largest such delta on the East Coast and includes spectacular areas such as the Santee Swamp, Santee Delta Wildlife Management Area and the barrier islands of Cape Romain. From its southernmost trailhead — the terminus at the Intracoastal Waterway and Bulls Bay — the Awendaw Passage overlooks a portion of this delta.

The Santee Cooper lake system is an intriguing man-made feature that has influenced the Coastal Plain and includes the Santee National Wildlife Refuge. Sparkleberry Swamp, because of the

Francis Marion National Forest:

The sad, complex story of "longleaf" ecosystems

Roughly 300 years ago, Francis Marion National Forest contained a fraction of the 90 million acres of beautiful, ecologically-rich longleaf pines peppering the American Southeast. Today, the forest is an example of how badly humans altered the region — and how nature stepped in to aid with recovery.

The federal government didn't acquire a pristine wilderness in 1936 when it bought the land that would eventually become Francis Marion National Forest. In truth, lumber companies had virtually clear-cut all 250,000 acres.

In the late 19th and early 20th centuries, timbering was the main industry in Berkeley County. Lured by vast pine forests and cheap land, a handful of large timber companies began snapping up huge tracts and using sawmills, railroads and overhead steam skidders to deplete almost the entire region. But when the Great Depression threw them into dire financial straits, the timber companies convinced the government to buy the land and bail them out.

Since then, the Forest Service has managed it for timber, to protect watersheds and wildlife and preserve the region's cultural resources. However, the Forest Service also made some poor — though well-meaning — decisions.

By following conventional thought and actively preventing forest fires, it allowed the fast-growing loblolly pine to replace the logged-over longleaf. From the 1960s through the late 1970s, foresters thought the longleaf grew too slowly and was difficult to manage.

However, by the 1980s, the Forest Service realized that by abandoning longleaf — and preventing the forest fires so important to the region's natural cycle — it was also losing a number of animal species that needed the trees to survive. The Forest Service was beginning to change its approach when Hugo barreled through in 1989, felling almost every tree in the forest with a diameter larger than nine inches.

What appeared to be a disaster was actually a stroke of luck.

After clearing the roads and thousands of downed trees, foresters began using aggressive re-forestation approaches and fire management to re-introduce longleaf pine. Today, the region is on the road to recovery and far more ecologically diverse.

flooding of Lake Marion, has created a biological paradise of unparalleled beauty.

Some intriguing Coastal Plain occurrences are small, elliptical depressions known as Carolina bays. These small wetland depressions are so named not because they look like bays, but because of the bay trees usually growing around them. When identified on a topographic map or from the air, they are very distinct with a long, oval axis always running northwest to southeast. Scientists have identified approximately 500,000 of these bays from Maryland to Florida, varying in size from one to thousands of acres. Most, however, occur in North and South Carolina; two dozen of the 200 in South Carolina occur in Francis Marion National Forest. Yet for all scientists do know about Carolina bays, they still don't know why such depressions form. Various theories suggest meteor showers,

The Francis Marion National Forest also includes some 14,000 acres of swamps and bottomland forest, two hugely important facets of the Lowcountry ecosystem. Swamps serve as huge cleansing reservoirs for the adjacent uplands of the forest; water passes through the soil, sits in the swamp as reserve, and eventually flows into streams. At the same time, the swamps' thick vegetation provides a habitat for many plants and animals — especially migrating songbirds.

In Colonial times, the early settlers cleared huge areas of swamp for their rice plantations. The landowners used complex dike systems and canals to regulate the water levels in these plantations and you'll use some of these dikes to visit the swamps even today.

Along significant portions of the Swamp Fox Passage, the path is just a few feet above the water table. That means you can expect large areas of "ponding" after periods of rain and standing water elsewhere in the woodlands.

Inland swamps serve as huge cleansing reservoirs for the adjacent uplands of the forest. Though off the Palmetto Trail, Hellhole Swamp was once Francis Marion's stomping ground.

ocean currents and sinkholes although the most promising argues that the bays' unique shape formed because of constant exposure to southwesterly winds. An excellent example of a preserved Carolina Bay (Dingle Pond) can be found near the Palmetto Trail's Lake Marion Passage on the Santee National Wildlife Refuge.

Elsewhere, maritime forests provide an important protective buffer between mainland and ocean. And while some of these forests are inland — the rim of Francis Marion National Forest includes several hundred acres of maritime forest — most exist on barrier islands such as Bull Island on Cape Romain National Wildlife Refuge, just off the Palmetto Trail. These forests are especially important to the Coastal Plains because they provide habitat for animals such as osprey, red wolf and great-horned owl. The Palmetto Trail also skirts important terrain such as salt marsh

DETOURS

Santee Limestone

When the famous British geologist Sir Charles Lyell visited the Lowcountry in January 1842, he didn't need long to identify the underground bedrock. Lyell named the rock "Santee Limestone" and dated it to the Eocene era.

Over the course of millions of years, solution of this rock has formed sinks and subsurface caves. Eutaw Springs — now flooded by Lake Marion — even originated from these underground channels. The limestone is used locally as a source of lime and amateur archaeologists might enjoy picking through the stone for fossils of marine animals.

A few miles south of Eutaw Springs, an impure limestone called Cooper Marl overlays the bedrock. This marl, together with the limestone, are basic materials used in the Portland cement manufactured nearby. If you can't identify the rock itself, at least make sure you can tell people what all those trucks are doing!

the Francis Marion National Forest, there are significant portions that traverse wetlands and standing water. The remainder of the Palmetto Trail delves into the sandy, dry soils of the upper Coastal Plain. The Eutaw Springs Passage includes pine forests and swampy, wildlife management areas supervised by the S.C. Dept. of Natural Resources. Before Hurricane Hugo, large portions of the area were mature hardwood forest. However, the powerful storm knocked down most of those trees and nature has replaced them with fast-growing loblolly and longleaf pine.

Wildflowers to Wildlife

Great blue herons, bobcats, Spanish moss and cabbage palmetto might not sound particularly exotic to native Charlestonians. But the rest of us have a real treat in store. The Coastal Plain portion of the Palmetto Trail offers exposure to flora and fauna you're not likely to see elsewhere in such abundance.

The red-cockaded woodpecker might rank as the most treasured Lowcountry inhabitant since the endangered bird only

and beaches — symbols of Coastal Plain living. Perhaps nothing symbolizes the coast better than the marshes full of shellfish, cordgrass and gorgeous wading birds.

Once it leaves the Francis Marion National Forest near Bonneau, the Palmetto Trail meanders around the man-made Lake Moultrie along the dike system constructed to hem in the water. The land here is generally flat and usually only a couple of feet above the water table. Just as within

These golden cinnamon ferns flourish under a canopy of longleaf pine.

nests in a few other places. Still, it's only one of 300 species of migratory and local birds that make their home in Francis Marion National Forest. Yes, this place offers true paradise to birding enthusiasts. Fortunately, that's not all either; amateur botanists and herpetologists will have a field day. Even if you're just hoping to spot a white-tailed deer or gray fox early one fall morning, there are plenty of opportunities.

The Sewee Visitor and Environmental Education Center on US 17 in Awendaw is the ideal place to begin your exploration of the Coastal Plain. Until then, here's a taste of the local fare:

Weeds, Grass and Ivy

Hundreds of years of farming, residential development and road construction has left significant tracts of Coastal Plain land sour, shabby and overrun with troublesome weeds. Interestingly, though, many of these weeds flare with bright yellows and purples during their flowering season. In the summer, for instance, the common yellow buttercup, red sorrel and purple spiderwort grows beside many rural highways. Elsewhere, in the deep woods — especially the dense, wet pine forests of Francis Marion National Forest — bluestem grass (commonly called broomsedge) dominates the ground cover. It shares space with toothache grass, plumegrass and common grass-pink, which is frequent along the Swamp Fox and Lake Moultrie Passages. These coarse weed-like grasses sometimes have flowering stems up to seven feet tall. In the salt marshes, spartina (or cordgrass) grows in abundance.

No other plants cause quite as much hardship as poison ivy and poison oak,

In the Lowcountry, each season produces a profusion of color such as sneezeweed, coreopsis and golden aster.

so any visitor to the Lowcountry should prepare to deal with them. You can identify poison ivy by its notched three-leaf pattern and tendency to spread throughout woodlands and meadows. The three-leaved poison oak looks similar to ivy but tends to grow more like a shrub, especially in dry, piney woodlands.

Wildflowers and Orchids

In the fall, the brilliant purple blazing star spreads through sandy woods of the coastal plain like a beacon. It's just one of several dozen attention-grabbing white, purple or yellow wildflowers that will pique the interest of amateur botanists along the Palmetto Trail. Three of four seasons offer color, too, from the butterfly pea of spring to coreopsis in summer and golden aster in late fall.

The blazing star and golden aster are just two of the wildflowers from the aster family peppering the Francis Marion National Forest. Their late summer and fall blooms will help take some of the edge off a humid hike during this time of year. But they're not the only plants that show off in the heat. The school bus yellow coreopsis makes its home along roadsides and in ditches — in other words, places we don't often look for natural beauty.

In the swamps and bottomland forests, blue flag iris (also known as the Southern blue flag) emerges with a regal explosion during the long days of early summer. Although it's tempting to peg swamps as drab and colorless, even the most inattentive explorer will stumble across white flowers such as aquatic milkweed and perky lizard's tail. You may have to look harder, but the swamp rose and pickerelweed hide in ponds — with the elusive purple flower of the pickerelweed emerging only a few days each season. Meanwhile, the Carolina bays house a wealth of colorful plant life including bladderwort, fetterbush, carnivorous pitcher plant, white sundew and red bays.

Several species of orchid grow wild in Coastal Plain forests, including the orange-fringed orchid, which enlivens pine savannahs in late summer. Another popular orchid is the grass pink while the perennial herb meadow beauty blooms in late spring or early summer with a gorgeous purple flower that can grow up to several feet tall.

Shrubs and Trees

The huge amount of the Coastal Plain land covered in loblolly pine forest creates

Marshes hold small surprises such as this pond lily.

one obvious problem. "A pine forest of from about 15 to 40 or more years of age is a veritable biological desert," Wade Batson writes in his seminal work, *The Wildflowers of South Carolina.* "This is due to the fact that the dense canopy and highly competitive root systems of close-growing pines exclude most other forms of plant life during this period; and, since the pines offer little in the way of either food or shelter for animal life, few kinds are found there." Forest managers, however, have taken great pains to nurture the native longleaf pine population instead of the more aggressive loblolly pine — and that has helped diversify the shrub and tree population. And since Hurricane Hugo downed vast areas of pine in 1989, the Coastal Plain has been awash with new growth ever since. Nowhere is this more evident than on the public lands of the Francis Marion Forest and the Manchester State Forest.

The Coastal Plain's Upland forests teem with a deciduous shrub that sometimes grows up to six feet tall: the sweet pepperbush. The narrow white flowers of the pepperbush also flower in the summer if you're brave enough to suffer the heat while looking for them. Elsewhere, the stream banks and swamp forests also offer an excellent habitat for the ti-ti, or leatherwood shrub, that sometimes grows up to 20 feet tall and blooms in summer with small, white flowers. The deciduous, six-foot tall pink azalea also emerges in the spring with clusters of bright flowers. And if you're ever in a pinch for snacks — or know your plants well enough to plan ahead — blueberry produce their tasty fruit in the spring.

The variety of trees in the Coastal Plain pales next to the number of smaller plants, but there is more to this region than pine. Of course, almost everywhere you look the prolific, short-needled loblolly pine is battling for space with the long-needled, large-coned longleaf pine. The long-needled pine can sometimes grow to 80 or 100 feet high. These trees once dominated the Atlantic Coastal Plain covering some 90 million acres of land from southern Virginia to Florida and Texas. But the nation's timber interests took an incredible toll on these trees and our misguided efforts at preventing forest fires nearly did in the rest. Now, with prescribed burning and aggressive forestry practices, land managers are helping to revive the longleaf pine in the Southeast.

The sheer quantity of pine doesn't leave much room for other trees, but some hardwoods do very well in the Coastal Plain — especially in the swampy, boggy wetlands and the bluffs along rivers. Live oak was once abundant in the maritime forests, but Colonial settlers used its wood for shipbuilding. Elsewhere in the Coastal Plain look for hickory, American beech, tulip poplar, sweet gum, cabbage palmetto and the imposing bald cypress trees that give the swamps such a dark and mysterious aura.

Wildlife

From overlooks onto Cape Romain National Wildlife Refuge to the sandhills of Sumter County, attentive backcountry explorers could fill a tome with accounts of rare and interesting wildlife sightings along the Palmetto Trail. The surrounding area is alive with animal life… so much so, in fact, that you'll battle some of it during your trip. The insects can make any outdoor exploration in the area a test of your fortitude. Plan accordingly.

Similarly, you will be remiss if you don't pack a few wildlife-viewing essentials such as binoculars. Bird watching potential abounds throughout the area and if you're cautious, attentive and quiet, there's always the chance you'll encounter elusive alligators, otters and the rare bobcat. Locals sometimes whisper about long-tailed cats in the Francis Marion National Forest, but biologists

D E T O U R S

Sewee Visitor and Environmental Education Center

Located in Awendaw just over five miles south from the US 17 trailhead of the Palmetto Trail, the Sewee Visitor Center is an excellent place to begin your study of the Lowcountry's natural history. The 9,000-square foot facility includes many hands-on interpretive displays and tourist information for both Francis Marion National Forest and Cape Romain National Wildlife Refuge.

Some of the better exhibits at the center are three-dimensional maps of the forest and refuge, the Birds of Prey Educational Area and a Red Wolf Educational Area where center officials occasionally conduct popular wolf "howlings."

The center is open Tuesday through Sunday from 9 a.m. to 5 p.m. There is no entrance fee. For more information, contact the Sewee Visitor and Environmental Education Center at 5821 US 17 N, Awendaw, SC 29429 (843) 928-3368.

don't deign to recognize their existence. Still, some people who claim to having seen one will argue tooth and nail that these beautiful and elusive animals do exist.

Birds

Francis Marion National Forest alone is home to some 300 species of birds, both migratory and non-migratory. A short list includes Coopers hawk, great-horned owl, great egret, summer tanager, pileated woodpecker, prothonotary warbler, red-

Bird Watching on/near the Palmetto Trail

The Francis Marion National Forest, along with the Santee National Wildlife Refuge and nearby Cape Romain National Wildlife Refuge are among the finest bird watching sites in the country because of the many species found in the area and an almost unparalleled migrating population. In the forest alone, biologists have documented nearly 300 species of migratory and non-migratory birds. Cape Romain was established in 1932 as a migratory bird refuge and the Santee National Wildlife Refuge in 1941.

Although you can spot many species by merely walking the Palmetto Trail, we suggest traveling to additional nearby sites if you're a true birding enthusiast. Some of the best include:

South Tibwin/North Tibwin Plantation off US 17, where five different habitats attract songbirds, wading birds, waterfowl and birds of prey.

I'on Swamp Reservoir, also off US 17 via FS 228, where taking a two-mile loop trail into the swamp all but guarantees you will see great blue herons and numerous songbirds.

Sandy Beach Wildlife Management Area, a series of dirt roads off the Lake Moultrie Passage, where you can get reasonably close to a bald eagle's nest and additional waterfowl.

Cape Romain National Wildlife Refuge, accessed by ferryboat from Moore's Landing. Almost any exploration on Bull Island will put you in sight of birds such as osprey, wood stork, northern harrier, great horned owl, terns and whelks.

Spur Trail at Eutaw Springs is a white-blazed spur off the main trail open from March 2 through September 30. This trail offers excellent bird watching along the shores of Lake Marion.

Santee National Wildlife Refuge offers a nature preserve of more than 15,000 acres of uplands, waterfowl impound-ments and open waters of Lake Marion. Managed for migratory waterfowl, a tremendous diversity of wildlife inhabits the varied landscape. Numerous hiking trails are available.

Sparkleberry Swamp consists of 16,000 acres in the headwaters of Lake Marion where the Wateree and Conga-ree Rivers converge. It's a true natural treasure, a gem brimming with wildlife, and a great birding site offering a unique outdoor experience for the paddler.

shouldered hawk and swallow-tailed kite. However, the most significant — at least to the Forest Service and other public land managers — might be the endangered red-cockaded woodpecker.

During the winter, migratory waterfowl flock to certain areas within Francis Marion National Forest and the Wildlife Management Areas bordering the Lake Moultrie, Lake Marion and Eutaw Springs passages. The Sandy Beach Waterfowl Management Area (unofficially known as the Santee Cooper Bird Sanctuary), for instance, fills with wood ducks and little blue herons. Elsewhere, you might notice migratory birds such as cedar waxwings, kinglets or yellow-bellied sapsuckers in the cooler months. Most of these birds are relatively common, but erratic in their wanderings and — in the case of the sapsucker, for instance — quiet, timid and easily overlooked.

Insects, Arachnids, Reptiles and Amphibians
Gnats, deerflies, ticks, chiggers…

If the mosquitoes don't get you something else will. Take your pick from among a variety of biting insects that make their home in the Coastal Plain, most of which fall under the annoying — rather than truly harmful — category of outdoor hazards. You won't likely spend much time inspecting the Coastal Plain's biting insect population and we're not inclined to do much more here than offer a few words of advice: Bring bug spray.

On a related note, the variety of spiders, amphibians and reptiles in this part of South Carolina is astonishing. Skinks, green anole (most people call them chameleons) and green tree frogs inhabit swampy areas and Carolina bays. Turtles such as the yellow-bellied slider and painted turtle lounge in dark ponds and wetlands. Meanwhile, you can find an assortment of flatwood salamanders spread throughout

both the Upland forests and swamps.

There are six species of poisonous snakes in South Carolina, but the ones you'll probably see while hiking include the harmless black and white Eastern king snake and (primarily black) rat snake. Still, poisonous snakes such as the copperhead, cottonmouth and canebrake rattlesnake do live in the forest. They most commonly inhabit debris piles, stumps and brush far from most human activity.

If you're both quiet and fortunate, you may encounter the reclusive American alligator along the banks of a pond or crossing a trail in the swampier regions. These creatures' aggressive reputation precedes them, although we shouldn't take them lightly — they grow up to 12 feet long. You'll usually find them in fresh or mildly brackish water.

Mammals

Hunting is a popular form of recreation in the Coastal Plain for a reason. There are more white-tailed deer, rabbits, raccoons and squirrels in these woods than you might think. Fox squirrels, bobcats and gray foxes also roam nearby.

And while the chances of seeing one are infinitesimally small, forest managers have documented black bear visits across the Coastal Plain. Usually they're foraging through shrubs native to Carolina bays. Don't count on seeing any bears, though.

Finally, although you can only see them in enclosures at Sewee Visitor and Environmental Education Center, scientists are trying to re-introduce the red wolf to this region. The folks at Sewee often conduct presentations about the story of red wolves in the Southeast.

Treading Lightly

Some wildflowers and small lizards of the Coastal Plain look so harmless and intriguing that we're occasionally inclined

Red-cockaded Woodpeckers

The seven-inch long red-cockaded woodpecker is only slightly larger than a bluebird. But this Coastal Plain resident is among the most important animals in the region.

Before Hurricane Hugo, Francis Marion National Forest contained the world's most concentrated population of red-cockaded woodpeckers — some 477 colonies. But when Hugo felled all the old, live pine trees that contained their nesting cavities, it dealt the woodpeckers a severe blow. Forest Service biologists estimate the storm destroyed some 87 percent of all active colonies.

In the two decades since Hugo, however, the Forest Service has helped the woodpeckers accomplish a startling recovery. With help from N.C. State University, the Forest Service began creating artificial nests throughout the forest by inserting wooden boxes in some trees and using a chain saw and drill to hollow out other trees.

Today, visitors can see red-cockaded woodpeckers throughout the forest. Biologists marked some trees containing live birds with two white bands, although you can also identify the cavities by large amount of white sap around the cavity's edge. Researchers think the sap provides protection from predators such as snakes since they can't climb through the sap.

You can identify the woodpeckers themselves by the black feathers on its back and head and white cheeks. It also has horizontal rows of white spots across its back. Males have a small white streak above the cheek, which you'll probably only see with binoculars. The birds — who live in "clans" — nest between late April and July.

In Francis Marion National Forest, the Forest Service identifies trees with red-cockaded woodpecker nests with bands of white paint.

to carry one home. Don't. Removing native vegetation from public lands is illegal, but it's also generally considered fruitless. The delicate orchids in these woods have a symbiotic relationship with their native soil that even horticulturalists have difficulty reproducing in the laboratory. The same goes for wildlife, which can't survive outside their habitat.

Additionally, Francis Marion National Forest includes four areas designated in 1980 as official "wilderness areas" with the intent of keeping human influence to a minimum. It is illegal to bring mechanized or motorized equipment into these areas. It is OK to camp, but there are a few spots where it's impossible because the forest is so swampy. Make sure to obtain a permit from either the Wambaw or Witherbee District Offices before you break out the tent.

Lowcountry Life: From Charleston into Santee Cooper Country

Though it deservingly remains the region's cultural heart, for our purposes Charleston merely serves as a launching pad for explorations into the surrounding Lowcountry. Much has been written about this 300-year-old city, some poetic, some far less so. For that reason, we won't spend much time here recounting Charleston's many attractions. Instead, we're more interested in the rebirth of other places

> *"(Charleston) is an object lesson, in a cynical time… of how, after a century of American travel that began with the European Grand Tour, we may yet discover that some of the world's prettiest cities are here at home, waiting to be reborn."*
>
> - Conde Nast Traveler, Sept. 1997.

throughout the Lowcountry: Think trinket shopping in Eutawville, bass fishing on Lake Marion and great food in Awendaw.

Exploring the Palmetto Trail will help you crack open a wealth of opportunity in an area just waiting for us to rediscover its getaway potential.

Charleston and Vicinity: The Hub

There is much to occupy your time in the city of Charleston, South Carolina's oldest and certainly most colorful town. From Charlestown Landing to The Battery and Fort Sumter, it's a quintessential Southern city, as elegant as it is historic. Its nickname is the "Holy City" for the many cathedral steeples overlooking street corners and markets — not for any virtuous inclination in the local populace. And the assortment of local restaurants, museums, carriage tours and shopping venues can — and do — fill up several visitor's guides.

So if you're planning a side trip to Charleston on a rest day from the Palmetto Trail, check in the references section of this guide for a selection of helpful travel books.

But for the all-too-brief, top five tourist attractions, try:

• **The Battery**: (a.k.a. **White Point Gardens**) Contact the Charleston Visitor Center on the corner of Meeting and Ann streets for more information, (843) 724-7474.

• **Charleston Museum**: The first and oldest museum in the U.S. It concentrates on interpreting the Low-country's cultural and natural history. (360 Meeting St., (843) 722-2996

• **The Old City Market**: Packed with small shops and restaurants, this market was built in 1841 and today serves as the heart of the downtown-shopping district. (On Market Street between Meeting and East Bay).

- **Fort Moultrie National Historic Site and Fort Sumter National Monument**: In 1776, Col. William Moultrie and his troops at Fort Moultrie withstood a cannonade from British warships, and returned enough fire to drive them away, too. You can visit the structure on Sullivan's Island for free. Call (843) 883-3123. Likewise, Fort Sumter might rank as the most historic military site in the nation since the first shot of the Civil War rang here in 1861. Daily boat tours embark from City Marina and Patriots Point Maritime Museum. For more information and fees, contact the fort at (843) 883-3123 or call (843) 722-1691 for boat tour information.

- **Magnolia Plantation and Gardens**: This 300-year-old plantation has been in the same family since Thomas Drayton arrived from Barbados in 1671. It includes the country's oldest garden, which offers spectacular color year-round. It's located off SC 61, north of Charleston and about 10 miles off US 17. Call (843) 571-1266.

Outfitters or Supply Stops

While you're doing a mad dash to visit the major tourist sites before hitting the trail, consider also that Charleston makes a great place to stop and pick up last minute outdoor equipment, food or literature. Numerous grocery stores, sporting goods shops and camping suppliers dot the city. But one of the region's best outdoor specialty shops is **Half-Moon Outfitters, Inc.** This camping and hiking supplier is now in two locations in the area, (320 King St. in Charleston (843) 853-0990; and, 861 Coleman Blvd. in Mount Pleasant (843) 881-9472). Stop by when the bottom falls out of a usually balmy Lowcountry winter day…

Food and Drink

There is no easy way to compile a selected list to great eateries in and around Charleston. The sheer number of excellent restaurants, coupled with the variety of food and local specialties just makes it impossible. But since we'll have to suggest something (and for what it's worth) this is a selection of four reasonably priced spots that add local color:

- **Anson** (12 Anson St., 843-577-0551) is a romantic seafood restaurant hidden off Meeting Street. Expect to pay around $15 for an entrée here, but the mostly regional specialties are worth trying. This is a dinner-only restaurant, although it's open seven days. The views aren't spectacular, but it has a nice, romantic ambiance.

- **Sticky Fingers** (235 Meeting St., 843-853-7427) has the best ribs anywhere. A relative newcomer to the Charleston restaurant scene, this popular restaurant morphed from a college project into an excellent stuff-your-face joint.

- **The Wreck** (106 Haddell St., 843-884-0052) is the scruffy gem of Mount Pleasant. Years ago, this rundown icehouse on Shem Creek truly was a locals' hangout. But word quickly got around about the casual atmosphere, large plates and excellent deep-fried shrimp and fish.

- **Jack's Café** (41 George St., 843-723-5237) is the archetypal breakfast diner. You'll find mouth-watering waffles, home fries and lots of good conversation from the locals.

Accommodations

Charleston consistently ranks among the top 10 U.S. travel destinations because of more than just the food. The city literally overflows with delightful seaside cottages, picturesque B&Bs, world-class hotels and even comfortable RV campgrounds. Unlike most cities its size, you can also find reasonable tent camping within driving distance. If you're going to pay for accommodations, though, consider shelling out a few extra bucks for an air-conditioned room during the summer.

You can find an excellent selection of Charleston hotels in some of the travel books within our reference section as well as South Carolina Places from the S.C. Dept. of Parks, Recreation and Tourism 803-734-1700, toll free 866-224-9339 or www.travelsc.com . For that reason, our list includes just one suggestion for the outdoorsy type who doesn't want to camp at a primitive trailside site:

• **James Island County Park** (871 Riverland Dr., 843-795-7275) Just a short drive across the Ashley and Stono Rivers, this excellent county park includes everything from a water park to an activity center and 50-foot, outdoor rock climbing wall. The tent sites are a tad expensive ($18 per night), but you get 24 hour security and roundtrip shuttle service to downtown or Folly Beach.

Must-See Sites along US 17 and Santee Cooper Country

If you're planning to explore the Palmetto Trail by using Charleston as the starting point, most of your trips will meander across the Cooper River Bridge and follow US 17 north through Mount Pleasant towards Georgetown. And while most of this land is the fringe of the Francis Marion National Forest backcountry, there's more here than meets the eye. There's just no easy way to say this: You're missing out by leaving Charleston and jumping right on the trail. The little fishing towns along US 17 offer incredibly enjoyable exploring and once you pop out of Francis Marion

National Forest to the northwest (near Moncks Corner), there are plenty of quirky local spots.

Likewise, Santee Cooper country is filled with hidden fishing holes and historic sites. Here's a look at some of the more popular tourist sites:

• **McClellanville**, which is approximately 40 miles north of Charleston, has a year-round population of around 325. But this quiet fishing village on the Intracoastal Waterway also boasts some of the region's most colorful history. Approximately 200 years ago, planters from the Santee River established McClellanville under the live oaks along Jeremy Creek. In 1989, Hurricane Hugo brought the town to national attention when the massive storm blew ashore here. It nearly leveled every standing structure — including the cafeteria of Lincoln High School where 1,200 people spent a terrible night. Although seawater from the storm surge reached a height of six feet, nobody was hurt. You can visit the high school and other local points of interest such as St. James Santee Church or just watch the shrimp boats roll in along the docks.

• **Berkeley Museum** in Moncks Corner traces 12,000 years of the area's history — from the Ice Age through the famous Revolutionary War exploits of Francis Marion. Inside, look for exhibits such as a replica of the CSS David — the Confederate torpedo-ram that delivered the world's first torpedo attack on the Union sub New Ironsides. The museum serves as a gathering place during American Revolution battle reenactments each November. "Living History Workshops" are also quite popular. Call (843) 899-5101.

• **Mepkin Abbey** is the original plantation home of Henry Laurens, the first president of the Continental Congress and a signer of the Declaration of Independence. But after the

Moncks Corner

Although it's tempting to suggest this town took its name from the monks at the nearby Trappist Monastery, however, most local historians trace the name to 1738 and landowner Thomas Monck. A valuable trading center from the beginning, early Moncks Corner included a handful of taverns and five or six stores. Most of the area's Santee River planters took their crops to Moncks Corner where they would sell them for cash or goods. The planters often dined in town and returned home later that afternoon.

In 1856, the Northeastern Railroad laid tracks over two of the area's former plantations and set up a depot and train station in downtown Moncks Corner. Workers restored the historic train station in 1999.

Today, Moncks Corner has two medical facilities, a population of over 6,000 and is home to Santee Cooper's headquarters. You can find most everything you'll need in this important stopover near the Palmetto Trail, from fast food chains to local favorites.

death of its last residents — Henry and Clare Booth Luce — the Trappist Order of the Roman Catholic Church took over according to the Luce's will. The Luces remain buried at the site which is now a beautifully tranquil monastery operated by the monks. Open daily. Call (843) 761-8509.

• **Cypress Gardens** bursts with wildflowers, azaleas and camellias. This 162-acre site is a black water cypress swamp wonderland. Hikers and bird watchers can see fantastic portions of the swamp, but paddlers might want to try a self-guided tour to get an up-close view of alligators, butterflies or wading birds. The gardens also include an interpretive center featuring a freshwater aquarium and butterfly house. Call (843) 553-0515 for hours and admission fees.

• **Francis Marion's Tomb** sits in a small clearing at the end of a long, paved road off SC 45 (between SC 6 and Pineville). Although it's indistinct and often overlooked, you can watch for a historical sign that marks the turn approximately six miles west of Pineville. Enter the gate and follow the road one mile along hunt club property to a parking area. Marion's gravesite is decorated simply with some fading flags, flowers and an iron fence. The land was once his brother's plantation, Belle Isle. No admission fee. Open daily dawn to dusk.

• **Eutaw Springs Battleground** was heavily developed when Lake Marion was built. But just off SC 6, about 2.5 miles east of Eutawville, you can find several historical markers and graves that commemorate this hugely important battle. On Sept. 8, 1781, British and American forces met here in the last significant Revolutionary War battle in South Carolina. Both armies lost approximately one of every three men and — although the battle was a draw — the British retreated to Charleston where they remained until they fled a year later. No admission fee. Open dawn to dusk.

• **Santee** literally sprang up as an exit off Interstate 95 when this heavily traveled road was first built in the late 1970s. Today, the town has become as much of a retirement town as interstate exit since the area is awash in fishing, hunting, golf and tennis opportunities. The Santee National Golf Club and Santee Resort help lure plenty of people, as do longtime restaurants such as Clark's. A recent issue of *Sports Afield* even named Santee as the "best outdoor sports town in South Carolina" for "out-of-this-world" fishing opportunities.

• **Jacks Creek** is said to be named after an Indian guide by the name of Indian Jack that traveled with the early explorer, John Lawson, as he explored the area. Today it's a favorite fishing spot for visitors and locals and a really great place to camp on the Palmetto Trail. You will find the folks at Jacks Creek Marina (803) 478-2793 will go way out of their way to accommodate you. During the American Revolution Gen. Francis Marion camped with 500 horsemen at Jack's Creek. A spy reported the camp to Lt. Col. Tarleton who lit a large fire hoping Marion would think that the Richardson mansion, Big Home, was on fire. But the Richardsons warned Marion who skirted the bogs and never checked Ball, his horse, until he had ridden across the dam at the creek. A Tory prisoner escaped and reported this to Tarelton and a chase ensued with Marion and his men escaping some 30 miles down the Old Georgetown Road.

• **Pinewood**, founded by the Manchester and Augusta Railroad, is located on SC 261 southwest of the city of Sumter and is said to take its name from the great number of pine trees in the area. You may want to take some time and poke around Pinewood to see what shops are open and don't leave without stopping by Linda's Grill for some real southern fried chicken and visiting with "John."

• **Packs Landing** near Rimini offers a large boat landing, supplies and some really great fishing guides. Call (803) 452-5514 for more information.

• **Wedgefield** in Sumter County was named from the fact that it forms a wedge-like approach to the High Hill of the Santee. Wedgefield is located on SC 261 between Stateburg and Pinewood. There isn't much

there except for Battens General Store and the Sportsman Kitchen (803) 494-8925 and some really friendly folks. You can get a good breakfast and a fine lunch or supper as well as an opportunity to thumb through the scrap books.

Outfitters or Supply Stops

There are predictably few outdoor outfitters along US 17 in Francis Marion National Forest or even in points north such as Moncks Corner and Eutawville. Most of the stores you can expect to find along these sections of the Palmetto Trail sell hunting and fishing supplies or the bare essentials for camping: bug spray, tarps, waterproof matches, etc… Still, it's possible to do a last minute re-stocking at some local stores.

• **Bulls Bay Supply** (10086 US 17 North, 843-887-3251) in McClellanville is an excellent general supply store. Owners Oliver and Debbie Thames stock everything from

---

D E T O U R S

The White Boots of McClellanville

Stroll through downtown McClellanville at lunchtime and you'll likely see lots of strapping fellows walking around in white rubber boots. Why?

Local shrimpers and fishermen wear the boots — usually turned down about halfway — on their fishing ships. It's one thing that identifies them as McClellanville shrimpers… sort of like a uniform. But don't do yourself any favors. You probably won't look too swell walking around in white rubbers back home!

lumber and plumbing supplies to sporting goods and no-frills camping equipment.

• There are a number of grocery stores and supply stops in Moncks Corner, but you might want to consider stopping by **Central True Value Home Center** (309 Rembert C. Dennis Blvd., 843-761-8588) for a good supply of camping equipment and outdoor clothes.

• **The Old Store and Museum** (1721 SC 35, 843-567-2255) in Russellville is another helpful general supply store. Owner Teddy Kieley keeps fishing tackle, hunting supplies and snacks as well as gardening needs, gifts and crafts. Locals also call this 75-year-old store the Harold Crawford Store or the Old Russellville Store. (Learn more about the Old Store and Museum when you read about the Lake Moultrie Passage.)

• The Lake Moultrie Passage passes directly past several conveniences stores and eateries in Bonneau Beach where you can get something you may have forgotten. You can find plenty of tasty snacks, plus camping supplies and insect repellant.

In the Santee Cooper region, Eutawville, Santee and along the north side of Lake Marion, you can find any number of landings, fish camps and/or marinas that sell little essentials and camping supplies. Before you go, call the Santee Cooper Country Promotion Commission in Santee for a visitor's guide. Try (800) 227-8510 (out of state only), (803) 854-2131 or www.santeecoopercountry.org

Some of the most reliable re-supply shops convenient to the Palmetto Trail include **Bells Marina** (12907 Old #6 Hwy., 803-492-7924) in Eutawville, which also maintains a popular lunchtime crowd. We'll talk again about **Rock's Pond Campground and Marina** (108 Campground Road, 803-492-7711) but

for now just know that you can find lots of helpful items here. **Duncan's Grocery** (Old #6 Hwy., 803-492-7686) is more of a convenience store, but owners Lacy and Mildred Duncan have been selling essentials such as flashlights and rain ponchos for more than 20 years. And **Pete's Quick Stop** (1883 Old Hwy #6, 843-753-7993) is a handy way station where the trail crosses SC 6/45.

The **Eutawville IGA** (225 Branchdale Hwy., 803-492-7579) is a converted cotton mill where you can also find most of your grocery needs just a few hundred yards walk from the trailhead at Eutawville Town Hall. The mill opened in 1942 but when Hugo slammed into this area in 1989, owner Bobby Bilton turned it into a grocery store.

Santee State Park (251 State Park Road, 803-854-2408) is a sprawling resort park near the Palmetto Trail where you can browse through gift shops, camp, try pedal boats and more.

Food and Drink

We can distill the food specialties on this portion of the Palmetto Trail into a handful of dishes: Fried shrimp, fried oysters, fried catfish, hushpuppies and barbecue. Healthy, huh? Well, maybe not. But man, this stuff hits the spot after a long day of hiking!

As with Charleston, there are many more interesting restaurants, lunch spots and diners than we have the space to mention here. But we can suggest a few particularly colorful joints that also happen to be convenient to the trail.

Once you leave the Charleston area and head north on US 17, one of your first stops could be the well-known **SeeWee Restaurant** (4808 US 17 N, 843-928-3609). It opened in the 1920s as a general store and finally turned into a restaurant in the early 1990s. The platters are relatively simple (fish, three sides and hush puppies) but anything fried here tastes particularly good, especially the green tomatoes.

McClellanville has a number of really fine eateries featuring home cooking and specializing in seafood dishes. Check out the **McClellanville Diner** (843) 887-4499 and the **Crab Pot** (843) 887-3156 both on US 17 and in "downtown" McClellanville the **Pinckney Street Kitchen** (843)887-4001 and **T.W. Graham & Co.** (843) 887-4342.

You won't find many eateries for the next 42 miles… until the Swamp Fox Trail emerges at the Canal Recreation Area off US 52 about six miles north of Moncks Corner. If you're doing a day trip, you have several options. **Gilligan's at the Dock**, formerly The Dock Restaurant, (just off US 52 on the Tailrace Canal at 582 Dock Road, 843-761-2244) is a seafood restaurant, RV park and bar that caters primarily to those who fish the Santee Cooper lakes. Gilligan's at the Dock has kept many of the fine old traditions of The Dock which had been an institution here since 1959 and it's locally famous for golden-fried catfish. Dessert pies (the peanut butter pie is a particular treat) are an excellent reward for a full day of hiking.

On the other side of Lake Moultrie, any number of fish camps and marinas offer meals, but many provide just your standard, diner fare. Though it's really just a roadside stand, **Mel's Grill** in Eutawville (803) 492-9334 has 18 flavors of ice cream as well as liver and gizzard baskets. You're definitely missing out, though, if you don't take the detour to **Sweatman's Bar-b-que** (approximately three miles outside Eutawville on SC 453; no phone). Even if you're through-hiking the PT, this barbecue joint is worth a six-mile walk. Of course, it's only open Fridays and Saturdays.

Accommodations

There are any number of hotels, fish camps and fee campgrounds near the Palmetto Trail and some really terrific tent sites overlooking the Intracoastal Waterway and the marshes. However, as in the Charleston portion of this guide, we're not going to make any recommendations here. Look for accommodations in South Carolina Places from the S.C. Dept. of Parks, Recreation and Tourism, (803) 734-1700, toll free (866) 244-9339 or www.travelsc.com

The brief list below covers the public campsites of Francis Marion National Forest and Santee State Park. There is more detailed information about campsites along the trail later in this guide.

• **Buck Hall Recreation Area** (Wambaw Ranger District, 843-887-3257) is adjacent to the Intracoastal Waterway and includes 14 campsites, a day-use area with picnic tables, grills and shelters. Directions: *From Charleston*, follow US 17 north for 30 miles to an entrance sign on the right. Buck Hall serves as the eastern terminus of the Palmetto Trail with connection to the sea.

• **Elmwood Recreation Area** (Wambaw Ranger District, 803-887-3257) is more of a hunter's camp since it also doubles as a S.C. Dept. of Natural Resources Game Check Station during hunting season. But this is a nice campground filled with live oaks draped in Spanish moss on the edge of the national forest at the Santee River. Directions: From McClellanville, drive north on US 17 for six miles and turn left (west) onto Charleston County S-857. Continue for 3.5 miles to the end of the pavement and follow the road (which now becomes FS Road 204) for 0.5 miles to FS Road 211. Turn left and continue to a stop sign where you will turn right into the camp.

• **Santee State Park** (251 State Park Rd., (803) 854-2408) is a huge, family-friendly state park on the shores of Lake Marion.

In the park, you can find everything from swimming and tennis, to camping and scenic boat tours. There are two lakefront campgrounds with more than 150 sites. Directions: From Eutawville, follow SC 6 northwest towards Interstate 95. Cross under I-95 and follow another three miles to State Park Road (Orangeburg County S-105). Turn right and follow to the park entrance.

Odds & Ends

There are many additional sources of information in the Lowcountry, from quirky newspapers to colorful radio stations and helpful web sites. We've included a few of them here.

If you're planning a trip to this region, it might help to contact one of these resources:

• **Charleston Area Convention and Visitors Bureau** (81 Mary St, 843- 853-8000 and www.charlestoncvb.com).

• In Berkeley, Orangeburg, Clarendon and Sumter counties, try the **Santee Cooper Country Promotion Commission** (US 301/15 and SC 6 in Santee, (803) 854-2131 and www.santeecoopercountry.org).

• The **Berkeley County Chamber of Commerce** (P.O. Box 905, Moncks Corner, SC 29461 800-882-0337) and the **Orangeburg County Chamber of Commerce** (P.O. Box 328, Orangeburg, SC 29116-0328, 803-534-6821.) Also, the **Tri-County Regional Chamber** (P.O. Box 1012, Holly Hill, S.C. 29059, 888-568-5646).

In Charleston, the Post and Courier is the newspaper of record. You can also find it on-line at www.charleston.net

On the radio, South Carolina is fortunate to have an excellent statewide network of public radio stations. The S.C. Educational Radio Network is popular in the Lowcountry where **WSCI** (89.3 FM) regularly hosts regionally popular programs such as the quirky Sunday night

music program "The Kitchen Sink" and Saturday programs such as "Blues in the Night" and "Vintage Country." There are several good commercial radio stations in Charleston, too, especially the ever-popular alternative rock station, **WAVF** (96.1 FM) and news-talk **WTMA** (1250 AM).

Getting Around

South Carolina's mass transit system consists of local bus service. There are no subways, and even the taxi services in most of the larger cities don't see exceptional use. So for most of us, it's down to three options: drive, bike or walk.

On the other hand, five major interstates crisscross South Carolina (95, 26, 77, 20 and 85), which makes this a very easy state to navigate. In the Coastal Plain, you will only encounter two: Interstates 95 and 26. You can use Interstate 95 to access most of the Orangeburg County portions of the Palmetto Trail, including cities such as Santee and Eutawville. Most other portions of the trail originate off larger secondary highways such as US 52 and 17A (in Moncks Corner) and US 17 in Charleston.

In the directions, we use five types of roads in South Carolina:

1. **Interstates:** These highways will appear as "Interstate 95" on first reference, later becoming I-95.

2. **Secondary Highways:** The larger highways such as US 17 or US 52 will appear as such in the text.

3. **State Highways:** In some cases, state highways allow access to the trails. Examples include SC 6 or SC 45 in Orangeburg County near Eutawville.

4. **Secondary Roads:** These roads are often indistinct or poorly marked, which can make finding some obscure trailheads difficult. In this text, we first attempt to identify all secondary roads with a road name (such as Steed Creek Road) and later with the country

road number (such as Charleston County S-133). You can usually find these numbers in white on black signs atop stop signs. Secondary roads are usually paved.

5. Forest Service Roads: In large tracts of public land such as Francis Marion National Forest, these roads allow access to recreation areas, campgrounds and obscure trailheads. These roads, identified FS 226, for instance, are usually improved dirt roads. These roads allow access to some very remote backcountry, so it's best to be prepared for anything when you're bumping down a Forest Service road.

Your experience will improve greatly if you familiarize yourself with various U.S. Geological Survey (USGS) maps in addition to any of the detailed commercial road maps available for Lowcountry travel.

D E T O U R S

Festivals

Labor Day in South Carolina pretty much signals the beginning of the social calendar. The Darlington 500 revs up, USC, Clemson and a dozen smaller schools start tackling in earnest and from the Upstate through the Lowcountry, hundreds of festivals celebrate okra, catfish, peanuts and more.

Fortunately, though, you don't have to plan a late summer trip to catch one. There are festivals year-round and some of them would make a fine diversion from hiking.

• **Grand American Coon Hunt** (Orangeburg/Jan.) The largest coon dog field trial in the U.S. Call (803) 534-6821.

• **Lowcountry Oyster Festival** (Charleston/Jan.) Buckets upon buckets of oysters. Call (843) 452-6088.

• **Lowcountry Blues Bash** (Feb.) Blues bands gather in Charleston. Call (843) 762-9125.

• **South Carolina Festival of Roses** (April) Edisto Memorial Gardens. Call (803) 534-6821.

• **Striped Bass Festival** (Manning, SC/ April) A special tribute to the Striped Bass and the Santee Cooper Lakes. Call (803) 435-4405

• **Hell Hole Swamp Festival** (May) A family-oriented gathering in Jamestown. Call (843) 257-2233.

• **McClellanville Shrimp Festival** (McCellanville, SC/May) Celebrate the Blessing of the Fleet and enjoy some of the local catch. Call (843) 887-3323.

• **Maize Days Festival** (Santee, SC/May) A family oriented fun filled weekend with activities, food, music, even a golf tournament. Call (803) 854-2152.

• **Iris Festival** (Sumter, SC/May) South Carolina's oldest continuous festival and ranked among the top festivals in the southeast. Call (800) 688-4748.

• **Awendaw Crab Festival** (Awendaw, SC/Sept.) Taste the delicious blue crab cooked by the talented cooks of Awendaw. Call (843) 928-3100.

• **Berkeley Antique Tractor & Engine Show** (Moncks Corner, SC/Sept.) Check out the horse power. Call (843) 899-5101.

Lowcountry Passages

Awendaw Passage

The Awendaw Passage connects the Swamp Fox Passage with the Intracoastal Waterway and the salt marshes making it a true "Mountains-to-the-Sea" trail. The trail follows Awendaw Creek and offers sweeping vistas of the salt marsh, unlike any scenery along the course of the Palmetto Trail.

The Awendaw Passage picks up where the Swamp Fox Passage ends just north of U.S. Hwy 17 in Awendaw. From there it cuts across US 17 to Awendaw Creek and jogs its way past palmetto and magnolia trees and through dense thickets of yaupon and gallberry bushes, terminating at the U.S. Forest Service Buck Hall Recreation Area.

"The Palmetto Trail!!!" Here is where you see palmetto trees. Most of the trail is in a tropical maritime forest with a predominance of palmetto, magnolia and live oak and loblolly pine trees. Bring your camera as there are really great photo ops around every turn. However keep in mind that while a very scenic trail, the marshy strip of tropical forest is a haven for a host of biting insects. The "no-see-ums" come out in late February followed by mosquitoes once the temperatures rise and the rains become plentiful. Snakes and alligators call the ecosystem home.

The trail winds through lands once part of Walnut Grove Plantation, actively cultivated until the mid 1900's. Before the European settlers arrived, Indians lived in the area and survived primarily off the plentiful shellfish along the coast.

Along the trail, bird watchers will discover a unique combination of shore and ocean birds. Herons and cranes mingle with wrens and warblers. On the ground, look for deer, turkey and fox. Even a warm day in the winter will bring out the snakes. You may even see a rare diamond-back rattlesnake.

Buck Hall Recreation Area serves as the eastern terminus of the Palmetto Trail and offers the trail user parking, bathrooms, water and information. A fee is charged for parking.

The passage is part of an overall outdoor experience. The Awendaw Passage is an excellent mountain bike trail. In fact it has been adopted by the local club for maintenance and improvements. In addition there are plenty of other recreational options nearby. The Sewee Visitors and Environmental Education Center is just south on US 17 along with the Sewee Shell Mounds nearby. A short distance to the north is the Santee Coastal Reserve. To the west is the Francis Marion National Forest with a quarter million acres of public lands and to the east is the Cape Romain National Wildlife Refuge with 77,000 acres of marsh, tidal creeks and beaches including Bull Island, an undeveloped coastal barrier island. A concession boat is available to the island. Call (843) 881-4582 for reservations, schedule and fees.

Buck Hall Recreation Area serves as the eastern terminus and offers the trail user parking, bathrooms, water and information. Camp sites are available on a fee basis but are worth the cost because of the spectacular view of the marsh. A parking fee applies at this site. The parking area is patrolled regularly by Forest Service law officers and a camp host is available.

Difficulty: Easy and very enjoyable but beware of the insects.

Length: 7 miles one way

Fees: Parking fee at Buck Hall Recreation Area

Conditions: June through September is the wet season and water can soak the ground along the trail tread. High tides close to the full moon in the spring and fall may inundate parts of the trail with brackish water. Tropical storms can damage portions of the passage especially the bridges and boardwalks.

Also remember that August through December is big game hunting season and turkey hunting season is in the spring. Wear bright colored clothing and travel in groups. Avoid red clothing during the spring turkey hunting season. High temperatures and high humidity can be a problem during the summer months. Biting insects along this passage are a real problem. The "no-see-ums" come out in late February followed by mosquitoes once the temperatures rise and the rains become plentiful. Mosquitoes will be present until the first frost in the fall and during the rainy season their numbers can be alarming. Deer flies are common in May and the bites can be particularly annoying. Snakes and alligators call the ecosystem home, including the poisonous snake varieties. Potable water is available at the Buck Hall Recreation Area

USGS Quadrangles: Awendaw

Directions: *For the Awendaw trailhead:* From Charleston follow US Hwy 17 north to Steed Creek Road (Charleston County Road S-1032) in Awendaw. Look for the trailhead and parking area on the left 0.25 miles past the intersection of Steed Creek Road. Traveling north, you will have to drive past the trailhead and make a U-turn at the next cross-over.

For the Buck Hall Recreation Area: From Charleston follow US Hwy 17 north to Steed Creek Road (Charleston County Road S-1032) in Awendaw. Three miles north of the Steed Creek Road signs will direct you to the right into the Buck Hall Recreation Area. It's a half mile down the road to the trailhead and the parking area on the left. Fee parking is available and you can pay at the fee station just as you reach the site. From McClellanville travel south on US Hwy 17 for 6 miles and the signs will direct you to the left. Follow the road 0.5 miles to the site.

Hours: Year-round. Night hiking permitted

Camping: Camp sites are available at the Buck Hall Recreation Area on a fee basis and offer a spectacular view of the Intracoastal waterway and the marshes of the Cape Romain National Wildlife Refuge. The campground is patrolled regularly by Forest Service law officers and a camp host is available. Showers are available for campers along with bathrooms, picnic table and a fire ring at the camp sites. Parking is permitted at your camp site.

Parking for day use at the Buck Hall trailhead is on the day use side of the

Camp sites are available on a fee basis at the Buck Hall Recreation Area but are worth the cost because of the spectacular view of the marsh across the Intracoastal Waterway.

recreation area to the left. A fee is charged but the area is patrolled and water and restrooms are available.

Information: Contact the USDA Forest Service, Witherbee Ranger Station, 2421 Witherbee Road, Cordesville, SC 29434. (843) 336-3248. Also try the Sewee Visitor and Environmental Education Center, 5821 US Hwy 17 N, Awendaw, SC 29429. (843) 928-3368.

On the Trail

The trail leaves Buck Hall Recreation Area from the picnic parking area on the left or north side of the recreational area. You may want to take a few moments and enjoy the view of the Intracoastal Waterway and the marshes beyond. The beginning is marked with a brown sign and the boardwalk that encircles the Palmetto Tree is a great photo opportunity for you and your group. The trail ducks into the maritime forest and if the mosquitoes don't carry you off then you are in for a really delightful hike. Crossing the main road to the campground and skirting the overflow parking you soon cross an elevated walkway through a wet pine forest bog. The blue flag iris will be blooming in the spring and are quite striking.

The overflow parking will fill up in the fall with trucks and boat trailers of recreational shrimp baiters. The boat ramp at the site is busy during the baiting season. Strictly regulated, the shrimpers catch their limit and make room for the next boat.

The trail meanders through pine forest, ducks under a power line and crosses a dirt road. Parts of the trail here are on private land. Users are asked to stay on the trail and respect private property.

You will cross back under the power line and head east back toward the marsh where you will soon reach some of the most scenic portions of the Palmetto Trail.

You are up on a low bluff with palmetto and live oak trees. The landscape opens up to the left overlooking the salt marshes. Short bridges or boardwalks carry you safely over the pluff mud found in the marshy inlets. The views along these inlets are spectacular.

You are now away from the noises of highway traffic and it has been replaced with the occasional drone of watercraft traveling the Intracoastal Waterway. Sometimes you will get to see the boats in plain view and other times you will only see the tops of the masts.

If you are lucky you will see some of the wildlife and if not, just look up and there should be plenty of bird life flying along. The bird life is a great mix of shore and land birds. Raccoons, opossums, rabbits, foxes and even a white-tailed deer may dart across the trail.

As you travel along look down at the soil along the trail. You will notice the many shell fragments left by animals, the tides or even the Indians that once inhabited the area.

The trail meanders along the edge of the marsh and often opens up to some really great views of the marsh and the

The Awendaw Passage follows a low bluff along Awendaw Creek and offers sweeping vistas of the salt marshes, unlike any scenery along the course of the Palmetto Trail.

Intracoastal Waterway off in the distance. The live oak and palmetto trees make for some impressive pictures. To your right the dense forest closes in and appears almost impenetrable. This is a true maritime tropical forest.

You will soon come to an impressive bridge over an inlet. Once used as a water control structure for a waterfowl impoundment, you can see some of the old pilings below. The bridge is made of a composite material and should remain structurally strong for many decades.

Further along there will be a number of small bridges and boardwalks all built by volunteers with the American Hiking Society. Each of these structures offers great views both to the right and the left.

Soon you will come to a place where the Awendaw Creek is next to the low bluff. Here a small live oak tree hugs the bank and shows the weathering of time from the harsh coastal environment.

Ground seepage can be a problem in some areas but a lot of work has gone into stabilizing the soils and allowing for proper drainage. You will soon emerge into an opening along a power line. The overhead forest canopy will now open and allow for great bird watching. Some really nice boardwalks carry you over the marsh inlets and the sticky pluff mud below.

The trail soon makes a sharp right and leaves the creek, crosses a paved road (Rosa Green Road) and then US Hwy 17. Once back in the woods the soil can be wet and the vegetation now more resembles a bog. Emerging on a FS gravel road the trail will follow the road for 0.3 of a mile and turn sharp left.

Crossing another paved road the trail is utilizing an old abandoned tram once used by trains moving logs from the forest over a century ago.

At the intersection with the Swamp Fox Passage you can proceed right along the Swamp Fox trail or turn back to the left and emerge out at the trailhead on US Hwy 17 near the Steed Creek Road.

People and Places

McCellanville and Awendaw are small communities along the coast with strong ties to fishing and the shellfish industry. McClellanville was founded by rice planters after their summer colony at the mouth of the Santee River was destroyed by the hurricane of 1822. Before long it became a year-round community and is home to many descendants of the rice planters. Today, the main economic activity is commercial fishing. McClellanville is located on Jeremy Creek and is home port for a large fleet of shrimp boats.

Both McClellanville and Awendaw are located within the African-American Coastal Heritage Trail. Almost every aspect of the area culture has been defined by the African-American influence. The story of the Carolina coast can still be enjoyed today in the food, folk tales, people and traces of history that have been left behind.

The freshening sea breeze blowing in from the ocean is considered healthful and is quite relaxing as it rustles through the maritime tropical forest. The area is essentially unspoiled and quite diverse. Outdoor enthusiasts are in for a real treat.

• Sewee Visitor and Environmental Education Center
A must stop to get your bearings.

This beautiful nature and visitors center is the headquarters for information to the Francis Marion National Forest and the Cape Romain National Wildlife Refuge. Red wolves can be seen in the enclosure behind the center from the Nebo Nature Trail boardwalk. Here you can get information about festivals and activities in the local area. Call for information on

Maritime Forests

Have you ever noticed the peculiar sculptured shape of the tops of trees and shrubs along the dunes at the ocean? Little would one realize that these plant communities are a complex ecosystem resulting from strong winds, sandy soil, low nutrients, sand blasting and oceans storms. They are maritime tropical forests and are composed of plants adapted to withstand these conditions.

These narrow bands of forests developed almost exclusively on the back sides of stabilized sand dunes. They occur along the entire South Carolina coast and are interrupted only by natural features like inlets and bays. They are dense but often open up to sweeping views of the ocean and coastal marshes. These forests serve as a protective barrier between the mainland and the ocean.

They are generally dominated by evergreen-broad leaved trees and shrubs. The composition of the plant communities is heavily influenced by salt spray from the ocean. Tolerance to salt spray is found to be the main factor that controls the vegetative cover in the maritime forests.

Fire has played a major role in the vegetative cover patterns in the maritime forests. The resulting leaf cover on the forest floor varies from pine to oak and plays a role in influencing the species composition as a result of wild fires. The composition changes are noticeable as one travels along the trail.

The diversity of the vegetative composition live oak/palmetto communities as well as the magnolia/hickory/holly communities are the result of complex conditions. Hiking in the maritime forest is truly an ecological experience.

Many different species of birds and animals make their home in the dense forest. Common are herons, egrets, pelicans, ducks and warblers. Birds of prey such as hawks and eagles utilize the area for feeding, roosting and nesting. Mammals such as rabbits, bobcats, mice, rats and even otters thrive in the habitat. Reptiles include turtles, snakes, the eastern diamondback rattlesnake, as well as a variety of skinks and lizards.

The peculiar sculptured shape of the tops of trees and shrubs in the maritime forest along the coast are the results of environmental factors affecting plants that have adapted to withstand these harsh conditions.

special events but expect to find activities almost every weekend.

Sewee Visitor and Environmental Education Center, 5821 Hwy US 17 North, Awendaw, SC 29429, (843) 928-3368.

• Francis Marion National Forest
A chance to wander the woods.

Just a few miles north of the historic city of Charleston, there's a 252,368 acre national forest located in Berkeley and Charleston Counties that's open to the public. Established in 1936 and named for the Revolutionary War hero General Francis Marion, it's the home of trees, plants, birds, animals; some rare and endangered. The

An impressive bridge over an inlet is made of composite material and should remain structurally sound for many decades. Views from the bridges are spectacular.

diverse recreational program provides excellent opportunities for campers, picnickers, boaters, nature viewers, anglers, and crabbers. Lying wholly within South Carolina's coastal plain, this verdant forest boasts a rich variety of wildlife habitat and offers excellent opportunities for bird-watching, nature study, photography, and fishing. Otters, beavers, coyotes, bobcats, black bears, and possibly even panthers make their home in the Francis Marion.

For those who really want to rough it, the Francis Marion encompasses four wilderness areas with no facilities except for a single trail. Travel through these areas isn't easy but offers extraordinary rewards, such as the chance to see alligators, bald eagles, and some 250 species of birds. A word of caution: Summer brings punishing heat and humidity and more soul-sucking bug life than you'll want to deal with. However the summer wildflowers may counter the insects. Some visit instead in the cool of late fall through early spring.

Witherbee Ranger Station, 2421 Witherbee Road, Cordesville, SC 29434, (843) 336-3248, fax (843) 336-4789.

• Cape Romain National Wildlife Refuge
A trip on the wild side.

The Cape Romain National Wildlife Refuge is a 64,000-acre Class I Wilderness located in northeast Charleston County. It was established in 1932 as a migratory bird refuge and is accessible only by boat. Today, it is the largest nesting rookery for loggerhead sea turtles outside of Florida, averaging 1000 nests per year.

Stretching along the South Carolina coast for 22 miles, the refuge is an important rich natural resource. It is also home to many other endangered species, among them the American alligator, American kestrel, bald eagle, glossy ibis, least tern, osprey, peregrine falcon, and wood stork. On Bull Island efforts are being made to assist in the recovery of the red wolf population. Bulls Bay and the creeks behind Bull Island were reputed hideouts for pirates plundering ships along the coast. The remains of the Old Fort on Bull Island are believed to have been a martello tower built in the early 1700's. Stories of retreating British warships restocking supplies on Bull Island during the Revolutionary War, Confederate blockade runners using Refuge tidal creeks, and the Union troops destruction of the martello tower used as a Confederate powder magazine are documented. Two lighthouses still stand on Lighthouse Island. The first was built in 1827, and the other in 1857. Although neither is operational, they are still used as daytime landmarks for ships and fishermen.

In 1925 Gayer Dominick, a Senator from New York, purchased Bull Island with the intent of making it a private hunting preserve. He had the Dominick House built and made a lot of improvements to the impoundments to attract waterfowl. Then in 1936 he gave the island to the Park Service to become part of the Refuge.

If your destination is Bull Island, take drinking water and food, and wear comfortable walking shoes. Always remember to bring cameras and binoculars.

Any visit except on cold winter days requires insect repellant. Spring is the best time to visit the refuge. The Bull Island Ferry takes passengers to the island for either guided nature walks or for self guided tours. Call (843) 881-4582 for rates and schedules.

Cape Romain National Wildlife Refuge
5801 Hwy US 17 North, Awendaw, SC
29429, (843) 928-3368

• **Santee Coastal Reserve**
A must for wildlife enthusiasts.

Designated as an important birding area along the east coast, the 24,000 acre reserve offers both hiking and biking trails along woodlands and marshes. The Washo Reserve is a must see with wood storks and hundreds of eastern shore birds. The tract is managed for waterfowl but has numerous acres of highlands. Visitors are required to park at the information kiosk which marks the beginning of the trail system.

Santee Coastal Reserve
PO Box 37, McClellanville, SC 29458, (843) 546-8665.

• **Hampton Plantation State Historic Site**
President Washington dined for breakfast.

A restored Georgian style plantation house on the Santee River offers a unique look at rural plantation life and the African-American influence on the culture of the area. The 322-acre property was once the center piece of a coastal rice plantation. Open to the public but call ahead to tour the house.

Hampton Plantation State Historic Site
1950 Rutledge Road
McClellanville, SC,
(843) 546-9361.

Outfitters and Nature Guides
Explore the landscape.

Outfitters are available to help the visitor in reaching their destination and to learn about the rich local area. The Cat

The American Hiking Society volunteers have spent hundreds of hours building bridges and working on tread improvement projects on the Awendaw Passage.

Island Ferry Boat works as a concession boat taking visitors to Bull Island located in the Cape Romain National Wildlife Refuge. A leisurely 30 minute ferry ride allows the visitor to relax and enjoy salt marsh creeks, egrets, herons, pelicans and dolphins. Self guided or naturalist guided tours are offered of the "boneyard beach" and along some of the islands 16 miles of nature trails on Bull Island. Call (843) 881-4582 for reservations, schedule and fees.

• **Nature Adventures Kayak/Canoe and Hiking Outfitters, Inc.** (800) 673-0679 offer tours on land and water. Tours are led by trained naturalists and are an excellent way to explore the rich natural area. Tours take guests into blackwater swamps, salt marshes, Indian shell mounds, rice plantations and barrier islands. Call for scheduled tours or to schedule your group tour.

The Local Eateries
Dine with the locals to understand the area.

The area has several famous restaurants and diners offering a variety of delicious seafood right from the docks and caught in the rich estuary waters. The locals rarely leave town to eat because the food is always fresh and delicious. A great homemade "lowcountry" breakfast can be found at the **McClellanville Diner**, US Hwy. 17 just south of McClellanville, (843) 887-4499, as early as 6 am. The diner features "shrimp and grits" and a "seafood omelet" along with a terrific lunch and dinner menu. For great variety of home cooked meals and their famous southern red rice, try the **Crab Pot** on US Hwy 17 in McClellanville (843) 887-3156.

Buckshots is a local favorite. However it's relocating closer to McClellanville soon. Watch for their new opening on US Hwy 17 North (843) 887-3358, because here is where you can get a "real coastal tradition" of a whole fried blue crab.

In "downtown" McClellanville, you can get a quick lunch at the **Pinckney Street Kitchen** (843) 887-4001 in the heart of McClellanville's village and enjoy your lunch outside under a huge pecan tree. All of their food is freshly prepared and served up just like you like it. Homemade delicious sandwiches and baked goods are always a treat here.

Now, the local meeting place is **W.T. Graham & Company**, 810 Pinckney Street, (843) 887-4342. Established in 1894 as a supply house for the village, it's McClellanville's oldest business. Today you can get some of the best seafood, steaks, homemade soups and desserts anywhere around. Call ahead for hours and specials.

Fish, Seafood and Produce
The Bounty of the Land

Folks from many different places have eaten Bulls Bay oysters and claimed they are the "Best in the World." The village of McClellanville has been growing and harvesting oysters, shrimp, clams and fish commercially for over a century. The industry has been passed down from generation to generation and is celebrated by the local Shrimp Festival in May with the "Blessing of the Fleet" ceremony. Visitors can buy straight off the docks at local retail stores or by trying their own hand at fishing with local charter boats. Try either **Carolina Seafood Inc.** on Oak Street (843) 887-3845 or **Livingston's Bulls Bay Seafood** on Morrison Street (843) 887-3519 for the best seafood to be found.

You can try your hand at picking strawberries at **Patriots Farm** (843) 887-4010 on US Hwy. 17 north of McClellanville. They feature seasonal fresh local produce and the delicious strawberries. Here in the mild coastal weather the strawberries sometimes ripen as early as March. Also you must try the hot boiled peanuts even if it is a hot summer day.

Convenience Stores
Stock up on what you need

To meet your needs for supplies and provisions, a number of stores are available. **Bulls Bay Supply** at the intersection of US Hwy 17 and SC Hwy 45 (843)887-3251 in McClellanville is a complete supply store with foods, camping supplies and hardware. They also have insect repellants. **The Pantry** on US Hwy. 17 (843) 887-3977 and **McCellanville Convenience** on US Hwy. 17 (843) 887-3788 offer a good supply of provisions. If you are in Awendaw, then try **Manigault's Snacks** (843) 928-3599.

Local Artisans
Trades that have been handed down from generations

Many talented and well known artists make McClellanville home. Some were born here while others came to relax in the serenity and beauty of the landscape of the historic shrimping village. You will discover artists who create iron sculptures, award winning photographs, watercolor paintings, silk scarves, walking cane sculptures, oil portraits, sweetgrass baskets, and even hand-tied shrimp cast nets.

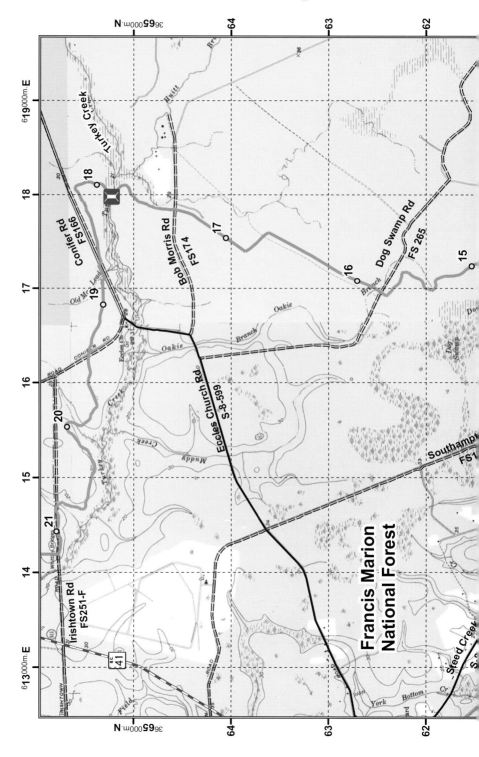

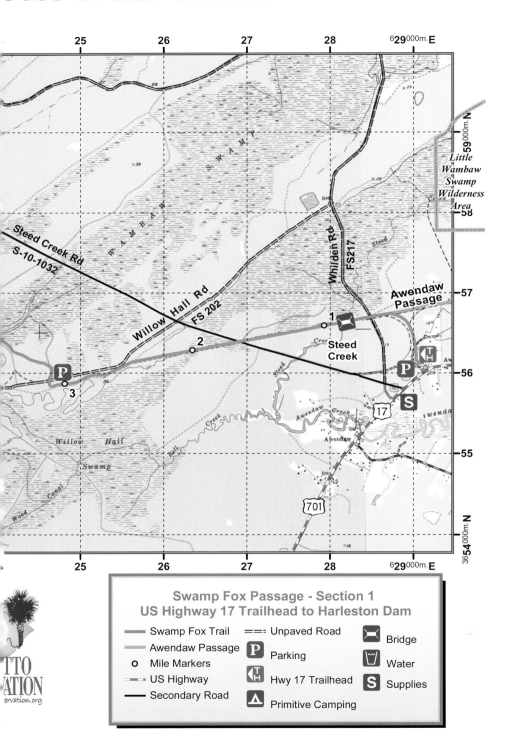

Swamp Fox Passage - Section 1
US Highway 17 Trailhead to Harleston Dam

— Swamp Fox Trail   === Unpaved Road
— Awendaw Passage   P Parking   ✉ Bridge
○ Mile Markers   🅷 Hwy 17 Trailhead 💧 Water
–·– US Highway   🅢 Supplies
— Secondary Road   ▲ Primitive Camping

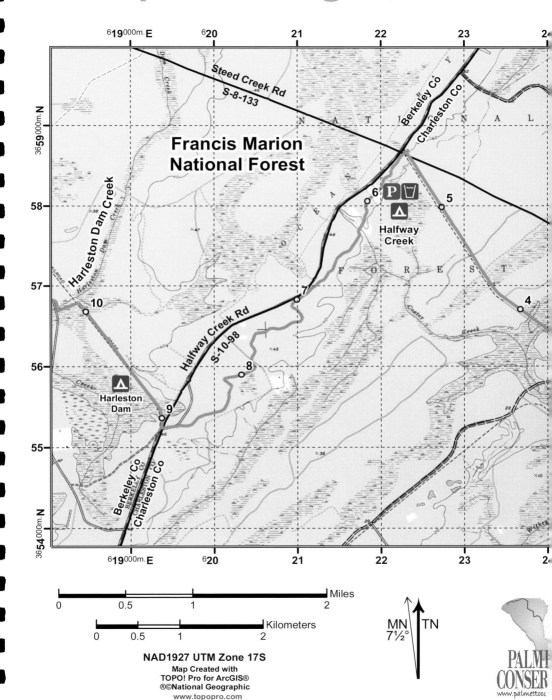

Francis Marion National Forest

Steed Creek Rd S-8-133

Halfway Creek

Harleston Dam Creek

Harleston Dam

Halfway Creek Rd S-10-98

Berkeley Co / Charleston Co

Miles
0   0.5   1   2

Kilometers
0   0.5   1   2

NAD1927 UTM Zone 17S
Map Created with
TOPO! Pro for ArcGIS®
®©National Geographic
www.topopro.com

MN 7½°   TN

PALME
CONSER
www.palmettoco

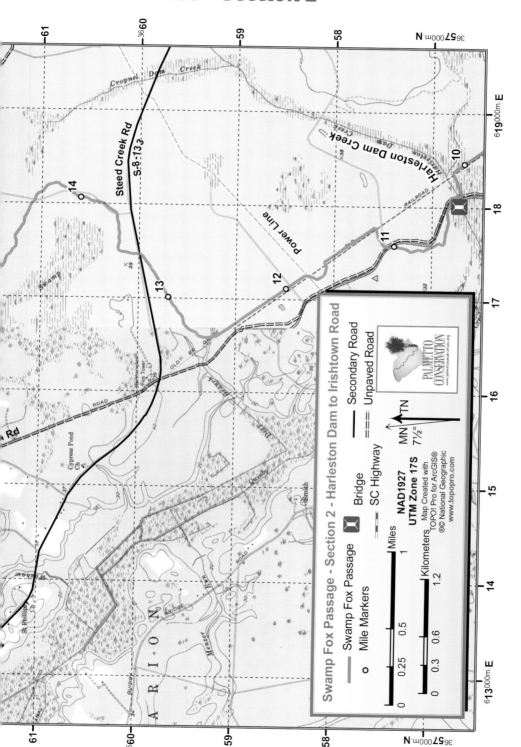

Swamp Fox Passage - Section 2 - Harleston Dam to Irishtown Road

— Swamp Fox Passage
o   Mile Markers

▨   Swamp Fox Passage
—   Bridge
—   Secondary Road
===   Unpaved Road
—   SC Highway

NAD1927
UTM Zone 17S

Map Created with
TOPO! Pro for ArcGIS®
®© National Geographic
www.topopro.com

MN   TN
7½°

PALMETTO
CONSERVATION
www.palmettoconservation.org

Miles
0   0.25   0.5   1

Kilometers
0   0.3   0.6   1.2

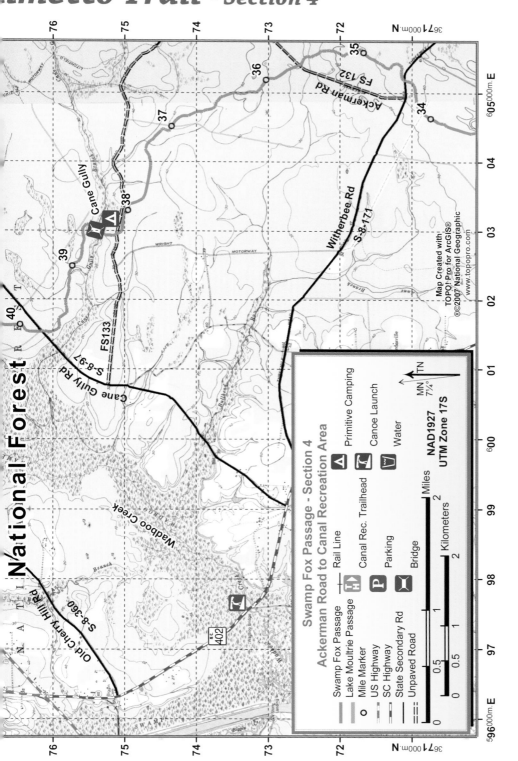

Swamp Fox Passage - Section 4
Ackerman Road to Canal Recreation Area

		Primitive Camping
Swamp Fox Passage		
Lake Moultrie Passage		Canoe Launch
Mile Marker	Canal Rec. Trailhead	
US Highway		Water
SC Highway	Parking	
State Secondary Rd		NAD1927
Unpaved Road	Bridge	UTM Zone 17S

MN 7¼° TN

Miles

Kilometers

Map Created with
TOPO! Pro for ArcGIS®
©2007 National Geographic
www.topopro.com

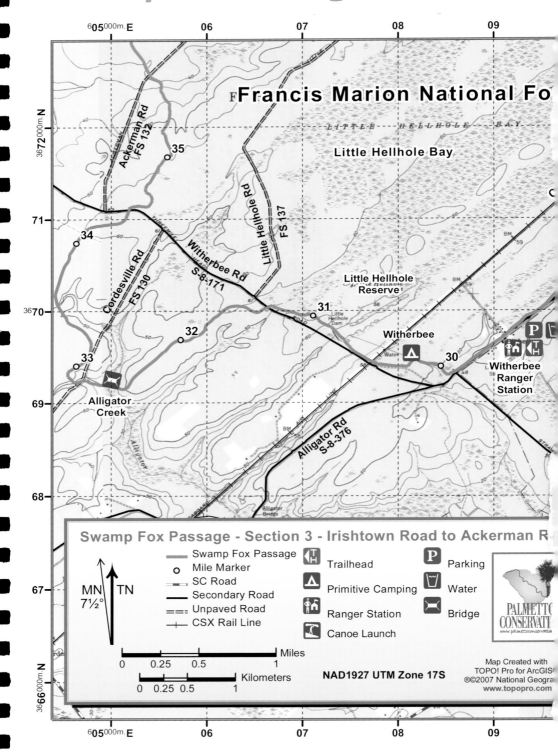

F Francis Marion National Fo

LITTLE HELLHOLE BAY

Little Hellhole Bay

Ackerman Rd
FS 132

○ 35

Little Hellhole Rd
FS 137

○ 34

Cordesville Rd
FS T-30

Witherbee Rd
S-8-171

**Little Hellhole
Reserve**

○ 31
Little
Hellhole
Dam

○ 32

Witherbee

Water

△

○ 33

30

P

**Witherbee
Ranger
Station**

**Alligator
Creek**

Alligator Rd
S-8-376

Alligator
Bridge

Swamp Fox Passage - Section 3 - Irishtown Road to Ackerman R

—— Swamp Fox Passage	Trailhead
○ Mile Marker	
- - - SC Road	△ Primitive Camping
—— Secondary Road	
=== Unpaved Road	Ranger Station
—+— CSX Rail Line	Canoe Launch

P Parking

Water

Bridge

MN **TN**
7½°

Miles
0   0.25   0.5   1

Kilometers
0   0.25   0.5   1

NAD1927 UTM Zone 17S

**PALMETTO
CONSERVATI**
www.palmettoconservatio

Map Created with
TOPO! Pro for ArcGIS
®©2007 National Geogra
www.topopro.com

605000m.E   06   07   08   09

3672000m.N
71
3670
69
68
67
3666000m.N

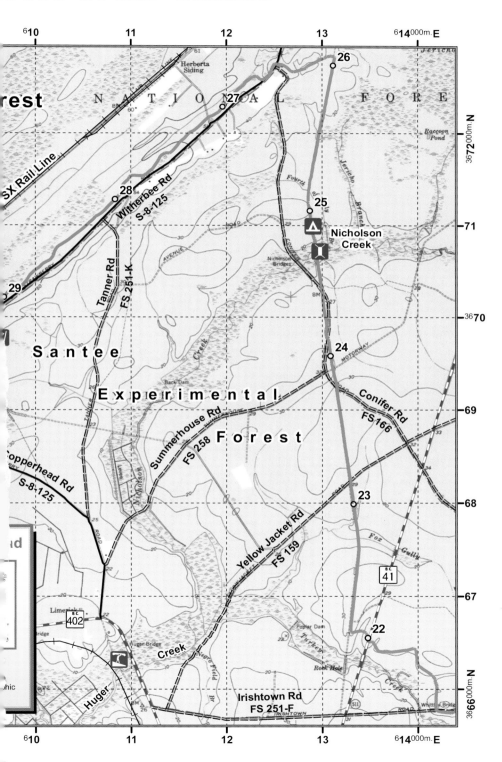

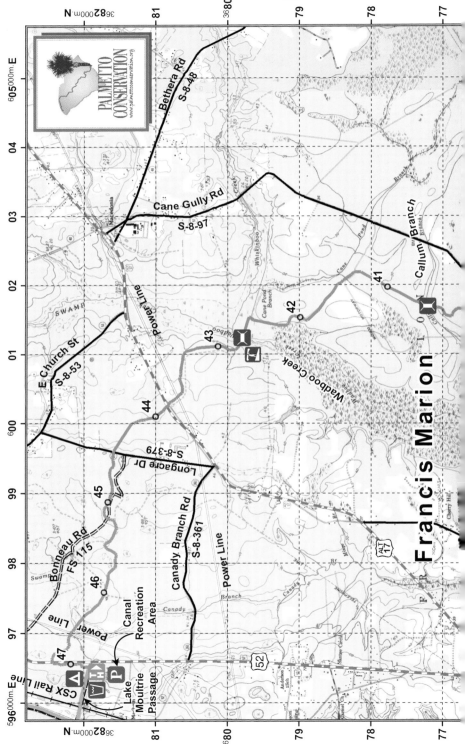

Swamp Fox Passage

When Gen. Francis Marion sought refuge from British troops by disappearing into the state's Lowcountry swamps — earning the nickname "Swamp Fox" — he probably never guessed the epithet would eventually define his stomping grounds. Marion's guerilla tactics and legendary reputation led Boy Scout leaders to name this trail after him when they built it in 1968. Today, it's also part of the Palmetto Trail. A 42-mile journey through four distinct ecosystems, the Swamp Fox Passage is currently the longest section of the cross-state trail. There are three trailheads, which means you can either do the trail as a three- or four-day trip or in shorter sections. Any access point makes for an enjoyable trip and diverse views. Of note are the gorgeous Wadboo Swamp near the western entrance at Canal Recreation Area and the grassy savannas around Dog Swamp and Turkey Creek.

Difficulty: Easy if done in sections as a day hike, moderate otherwise

Length: 47 miles one way

Fees: None

Conditions: June through August is wet season and water often stands several inches deep in large areas of the forest. Wear sturdy shoes that can withstand damp conditions and, if mountain biking, be prepared to ride through extended sections of mud, sand and standing water. Maintenance crews placed long log "bridges" over many of these ponds, but you'll be hard pressed to ride the narrow, slippery wood. Instead, simply walk across them pushing your bike. Some sections of this trail — particularly one section south of Halfway Creek Campground — are exceedingly bumpy because railroad crossties remain embedded below the surface. Also consider that August through December is big game hunting season. Wear bright clothing on the trail during this period. High temperatures and biting insects (mosquitoes, chiggers and ticks) can be a problem in warm weather. Potable water is available at the Canal and Witherbee Trailheads and Halfway Creek Campground.

USGS Quadrangles: Awendaw, Ocean Bay, Huger, Bethera, Cordesville and Bonneau

Directions: *For southeastern trailhead:* From Charleston, follow US 17 north to Steed Creek Road (Charleston County Road S-1032) in Awendaw. Look for the trailhead and parking area on the left (west), 0.25 miles past Steed Creek Road. Coming from the south, you'll have to drive past the trailhead and make a U-turn at the next intersection.

For middle trailhead: From Awendaw, turn left off US 17 onto Steed Creek Road (Charleston County Road S-1032) and follow 12 miles to Huger, where you continue straight through a blinking light onto SC 402. Travel two miles to Copperhead Road (SC 125) and turn right (north). Follow for another two miles to Witherbee Road where you will turn right (northeast) and travel 0.5 miles to the Witherbee Ranger Station parking area on the right. The trailhead is on the left side of Witherbee Road. (To reach this trailhead from Charleston, travel north on US 17 for nine miles and turn left onto SC 41. Travel 17 miles to the intersection with SC 402 in Huger and follow the directions above. To reach this trailhead from Moncks Corner, follow US 52 north to SC 402. Turn right and travel three miles to Witherbee Road where you will turn left and travel seven miles to the ranger station.)

For the northwestern trailhead: From Moncks Corner, follow US 52 north. Once 52 splits from 17A on the left travel another 3.6 miles to the US Forest Service Canal Recreation Area on the left.

Hours: Year-round. Night hiking permitted.

Camping: There is primitive car camping

A busy day at the US 17 trailhead for the Palmetto Trail.

available at Halfway Creek and there are several other backcountry sites along the trail. However, camping is limited to the designated areas. The cutting of live trees for firewood is prohibited.

Information: Contact the USDA Forest Service, Witherbee Ranger District, 2421 Witherbee Road, Cordesville, S.C. 29434. (843) 336-3248. Also try the Sewee Visitor & Environmental Education Center, 5821 Hwy. 17 N, Awendaw, S.C. 29429. (843) 928-3368.

On the Trail

From the Awendaw trailhead, skirt information kiosks and follow the narrow passage through dense pines, honeysuckle and live oaks. The Swamp Fox Trail is so interesting partly because it will occasionally round a bend and continues in a straight line for hundreds of yards at a clip. On these stretches, you are traveling along an old railroad right-of-way that keeps you high and dry. There's something unnerving about seeing such dense wood enveloping the trail and, if you move quietly, wildlife may dart across in the distance.

The trail crosses a small footbridge and Charleston County S-217 in the first mile, but the first major landmark is a well-built wooden bridge over Steed Creek at the 0.9-mile point. This is a nice spot for photography since the creek is dark and filled with bald cypress. The trail continues for 2.5 miles where you'll emerge into a

grove of new loblolly pine, many blown sideways by various storms. This continues for another mile until you pop out of the woods and turn right onto Cooter Creek Road (FS 224). The dirt road skirts Cooter Creek, then plunges back into the pine forest where some exceptionally heavy undergrowth often grows across the trail.

At six miles, the trail passes through Halfway Creek Campground, an especially convenient campsite since it's not far from the junction of Halfway Creek Road (Charleston County S-98) and Steed Creek Road. The campground includes a hand pump for water. From here, continue southwest into an enjoyable longleaf pine forest for the next two miles. The pines with white markings here contain red-cockaded woodpecker cavities.

Cross Halfway Creek Road and follow the trail past the primitive camp at Harleston Dam and a bridge over Harleston Creek before crossing Steed Creek Road again. The next eight miles include such highlights as the grassy savannah around Dog Swamp, remnants of a tar kiln used in shipbuilding, and a bridge through dark cypress and gum trees over Turkey Creek. These wetlands are among the lowest elevation on this part of the trail and often remain wet for weeks at a time.

After Turkey Creek, the Swamp Fox Trail runs concurrently with the Jericho Horse Trail — six miles open to equestrians.

Maintenance crews placed long, log "bridges" over many low-lying wet areas of the trail.

Hiking along the Swamp Fox Passage

Fortunately, the trail is somewhat higher here and extremely straight, although it crosses SC 41 one time and joins a railroad bed that skirts Jericho Swamp and occasionally crosses Nicholson Creek. Just beyond a swampy section of the creek, there is a primitive campsite (no water).

In just over a mile, the trail veers left and crosses Witherbee Road (SC 125) and continues uneventfully to the Witherbee Ranger Station.

From this access point — where you can find water — the trail skirts the fringe of Little Hellhole Bay, even crossing Little Hellhole Dam after 1.5 miles. This is the newest section of trail and (although clear and well-marked) it isn't always as worn as the original Swamp Fox Trail. It's also much lower, so you should avoid this area after periods of heavy rain. For the next nine miles, the trail follows a series of old forest roads, trail and boardwalk through grassy fields and over obstacles such as Alligator Creek. The trail passes Cane Gully Primitive Camp and pops out at Berkeley County S-97 before dropping back into the woods at arguably the best portion of this entire trail.

The next section runs through the dark and foreboding Wadboo Swamp. Finally completed in late 1998, this section includes over a dozen bridges and boardwalks that carry travelers deep into the swamp. The most significant is the Henry Brown Bridge, named for the 1st Congressional District Congressman. It is here you will find a put-in for the Wadboo Creek Canoe Trail. Access for the canoe trail is from the end of FS Road #199 off US 17-A just south of the community of Macedonia. You may run into anglers here, fishing for bream, bass or catfish under the dark waters. One portion of the trail also runs along an old rice paddy dike system.

After Wadboo Swamp, the trail continues across US 17A and into very low ground. Mountain bikers will find the going especially slow here since the ground is often very muddy and the narrow boardwalks won't appeal to inexperienced riders. The woodlands here are filled with sweet pepper bush, pipewort and blue flag iris.

Finally emerge at US 52 (which, like US 17, is a busy highway crossing) and plow up a steep embankment to rejoin the trail on the other side. The trailhead is Canal Recreation Area, which has pit toilets and a hand pump for water. There is another primitive campsite north of the canal, which we'll discuss in the next section.

The bridge over Steed Creek allows visitors to capture glimpses of rarely visited Lowcountry swamps.

People & Places

SeeWee Restaurant

From church to general store to scrumptious seafood.

4808 US 17 North,
Awendaw, SC 29429
(843) 928-3609

Named for a small, ill-fated tribe of Indians who inhabited the area before European colonization, the SeeWee Restaurant has been a local landmark for longer than one might think.

It's known today for simple, delicious Lowcountry fare, including – as one reviewer once wrote – seafood so fresh that the fishes' next of kin haven't been notified yet. But humans have used the site on which the SeeWee sits for centuries.

Located on US 17 just 10 miles south of the Palmetto Trail's Awendaw trailhead, the restaurant exists at a point long known as "Wappetaw." A small tribe of Indians roamed this area for many years prior to English settlement. Archaeologists think the Sewee tribe – which probably numbered around 100 – were the first to greet the settlement at Charles Town.

The tribe eventually disappeared around 1700 after most of its working-age men perished in a hopeless attempt to sail across the Atlantic and trade directly with the English.

Later, a group of New England colonists settled at Wappetaw in 1696 and built a church. The structure eventually fell into disrepair, although markers still remain on 15-Mile Landing Road directly behind the SeeWee Restaurant.

The current building was built as a general store in the 1920s and purchased by its present owner, Mary Rancourt, in the '60s. After watching several tenants come and go, Rancourt and her son, Kurt Penninger, converted the building into a restaurant in 1993. They decided to keep the store's old shelving, creaky hardwood floors and red tin roof.

Penninger, who still manages the restaurant and often works six days a week, said they used family recipes and local secrets to make some of the SeeWee's popular dishes.

"Mom's she-crab soup was always a big hit," Penninger said. "We just started making the food we knew… (and) the locals were the first to start coming in. Now we do pretty good business."

So good, in fact, the SeeWee sometimes overflows on weekend nights. Come early; there are no reservations.

Once inside, you'll want to check out the day's specials since they usually hinge on what the local fisherman brought home. All the seafood baskets are excellent and most dishes feature a main course with three sides.

"It's been one of our signatures," Penninger said. "At SeeWee, we've always liked giving people the opportunity to choose their side (dishes). A few other restaurants have gone to that style, too."

Hours: 11 a.m. to 9 p.m. Monday through Thursday; 11 a.m. to 10 p.m. on Friday; 8 a.m. to 10 p.m. on Saturday; 11 a.m. to 3 p.m. on Sunday

Price range: $4.50 to $14.95 for most entrees.

How to Pay: Cash/major credit cards

The SeeWee Restaurant was built as a general store in the early 1920s and operated as such for many years. Owner Mary Rancourt turned it into a restaurant in 1993.

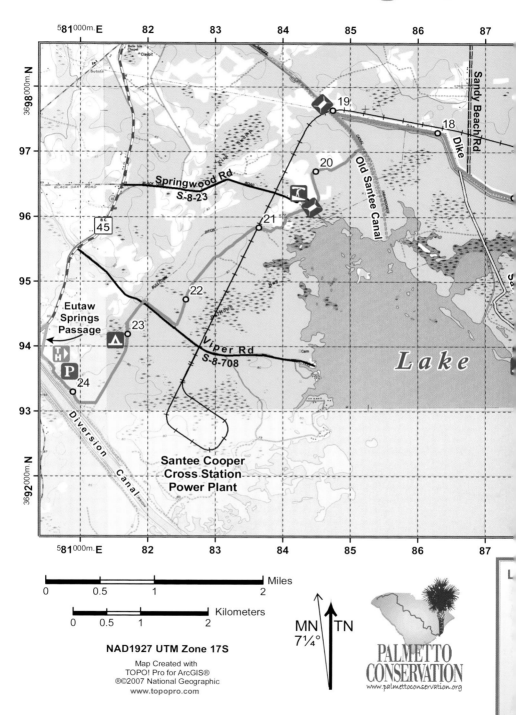

Santee Cooper
Cross Station
Power Plant

Eutaw
Springs
Passage

Springwood Rd
S-8-23

Viper Rd
S-8-708

Old Santee Canal

Sandy Beach Rd

Dike

Diversion Canal

Lake

Miles
0   0.5   1   2

Kilometers
0   0.5   1   2

NAD1927 UTM Zone 17S

Map Created with
TOPO! Pro for ArcGIS®
®©2007 National Geographic
www.topopro.com

MN
7¼°   TN

PALMETTO
CONSERVATION
www.palmettoconservation.org

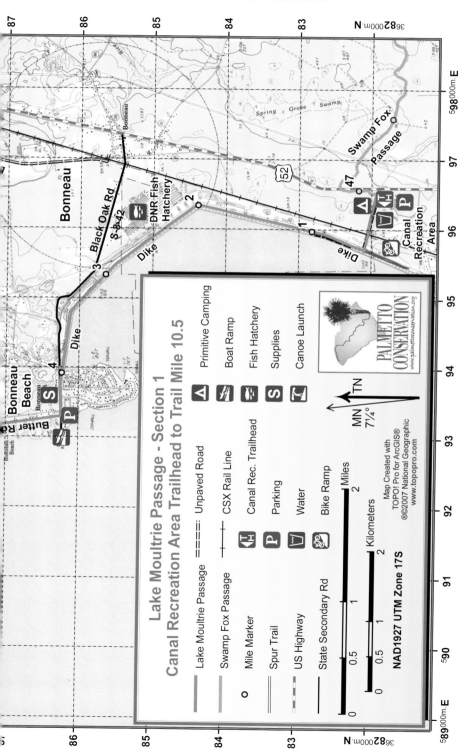

Lake Moultrie Passage - Section 1
Canal Recreation Area Trailhead to Trail Mile 10.5

Lake Moultrie Passage
Swamp Fox Passage
o Mile Marker
Spur Trail
US Highway
State Secondary Rd

==== Unpaved Road
—+— CSX Rail Line
Canal Rec. Trailhead
Parking
Water
Bike Ramp

Primitive Camping
Boat Ramp
Fish Hatchery
Supplies
Canoe Launch

MN 7¼° TN

Miles
0   0.5   1   2
Kilometers
0   0.5   1   2

NAD1927 UTM Zone 17S

Map Created with
TOPO! Pro for ArcGIS®
®©2007 National Geographic
www.topopro.com

PALMETTO
CONSERVATION
www.palmettoconservation.org

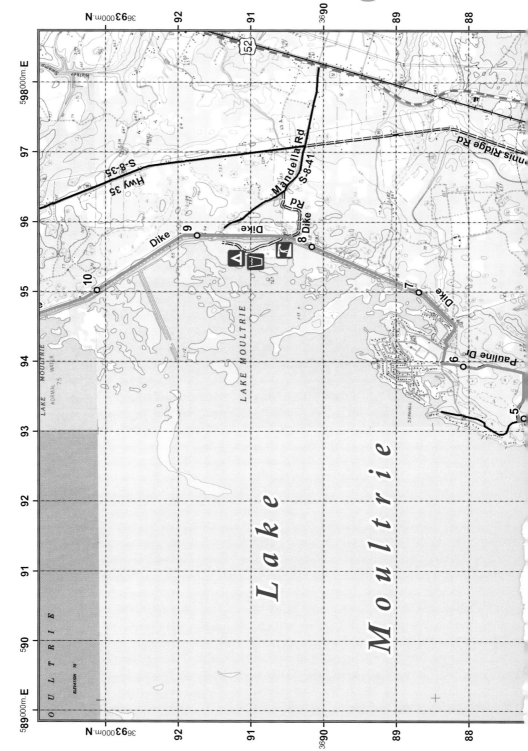

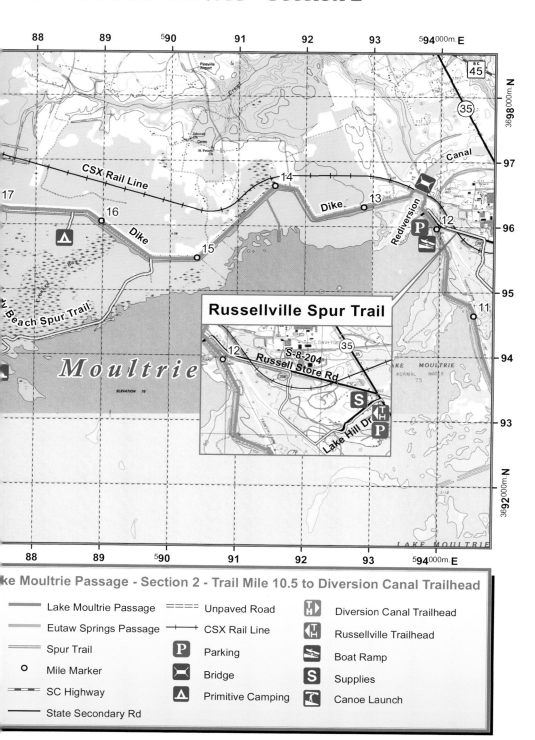

Russellville Spur Trail

Lake Moultrie Passage - Section 2 - Trail Mile 10.5 to Diversion Canal Trailhead

⎯⎯⎯ Lake Moultrie Passage	==== Unpaved Road	🚩	Diversion Canal Trailhead
⎯⎯⎯ Eutaw Springs Passage	⎯+⎯ CSX Rail Line	🚩	Russellville Trailhead
═══ Spur Trail	🅿 Parking	⛵	Boat Ramp
○ Mile Marker	✉ Bridge	S	Supplies
▦ SC Highway	▲ Primitive Camping	🛶	Canoe Launch
⎯⎯⎯ State Secondary Rd			

Lake Moultrie Passage

In 1996 this 24-mile passage became the first official segment of the Palmetto Trail. Flat, scenic and with two easy access points — each just a short distance from some remote and beautiful country — it's still one of the most popular, especially with mountain bikers.

The trail rings Lake Moultrie's eastern and northern shores via service roads along the lake's dike system. At the southern trailhead (Canal Recreation Area) the trail begins with a short stretch through a pine forest and climbs steps up the earthen Pinopolis East Dike. Here you'll get spectacular views of the lake, especially at sunset. The northern portion of the trail continues along the dike system until you cross the Old Santee Canal on an old railroad trestle. The last few miles of the Lake Moultrie Passage push through a mature hardwood and pine forest that includes some of the trail's most interesting terrain.

Difficulty: Easy if done in sections as a day hike, moderate otherwise

Length: 24 miles one way

Fees: None

Conditions: Generally good. Large portions of this trail traverse the raised dike system around Lake Moultrie where the footing is usually flat and dry. Some low-lying sections do tend to hold water. High temperatures and biting insects (mosquitoes, chiggers and ticks) can be a problem in warm weather.

USGS Quadrangles: Bonneau, Pineville and St. Stephen.

Directions: *For the southern trailhead (Canal Recreation Area):* From Charleston, follow US 52 into Moncks Corner and stay on US 52 straight out of town. Look for signs at the US Forest Service Canal Recreation Area, 3.6 miles from the split of 52 and US 17A. (From Santee on Interstate 95, follow SC 6 into Moncks Corner and follow directions above.)

For the Rediversion Canal entrance: From Canal Recreation Area, continue north on US 52 for approximately four miles. At a sign for Russellville, turn left (west) onto Mandella Road (Berkeley County S-41.) Continue 0.75 miles and turn right (north) onto Dennis Ridge Road (Berkeley County S-35.) After 2.9 miles, turn left (west) onto Berkeley County S-204 and park at the Russellville Boat Landing.

For the Sandy Beach Wildlife Management Area entrance: From the Russellville Boat Landing, continue on Berkeley County S-35 another two miles and turn left (west) onto SC 45. Follow SC 45 for five miles and turn left onto Sandy Beach Rd. Continue another 2.5 miles to

Santee Cooper employees spent many hours building the wooden bridges over low-lying areas of the Lake Moultrie Passage.

the dike and the edge of the WMA.

For the northern trailhead (Diversion Canal Entrance): From Pineville, continue on SC 45 another six miles past the turn at Sandy Beach Road. Just before a bridge, turn left onto Eadie Lane. Follow the dirt road past homes on the left for 0.4 miles to the second pullout on the right (don't park in the cul-de-sac with a fire ring overlooking the canal). Instead, look for small, yellow trail markers at a stand of pine trees and beside a fenced-in lot of quarried rock. Park here. From the pullout, continue down the dirt road around the rock pile and past large, kudzu-covered embankments.

From Columbia, follow Interstate 26 to Jedburg-Pinopolis (exit 194). Turn left (east) toward Pinopolis on Berkeley County S-16. Follow for 18 miles to an intersection with SC 6. Turn left (north) on SC 6 and follow past Cross to an intersection with SC 45. Turn right (east) toward St. Stephen. After five miles, SC 6 crosses the Diversion Canal. Take the first dirt road (Eadie Lane) to the right (south) and follow it to a parking area beside the canal.

Hours: Year-round

Camping: Primitive campsites with hand-operated water pumps are near the Diversion Canal trailhead and two spots in or near the Sandy Beach Wildlife Management Area. There is another primitive campsite 1.8 miles after leaving the Bonneau Beach community at General Moultrie Road.

Information: Contact Supervisor-Forestry & Undeveloped Lands, Santee Cooper Land Division, One Riverwood Drive, Moncks Corner, S.C. 29461. (843) 761-8000.

On the Trail

From the parking lot at Canal Recreation Area, look across the stream

The Lake Moultrie Passage of the Palmetto Trail begins with a short, steep climb up to the dike system encircling the lake.

for a large kiosk with trail brochures and interpretive panels. Join the obvious trail here and follow 0.5 miles west through a stand of pines and climb steps up the earthen Pinopolis East Dike. (Mountain bikers can reach the top of the dike by traveling south along the dike for 0.4 miles to an access ramp.)

From the top of the stairs, proceed north along the dike until it ends at Black Oak Road (Berkeley County S-42.) You can look south from the top of the dike and see the large stacks of Santee Cooper's Jeffries Generating Station. The next 2.2 miles are a temporary section across paved roads and through mixed residential and commercial area. It is somewhat confusing, hence the more detailed directions.

When the dike deposits you onto Black Oak Road, continue left (west) to Butter Road (Berkeley County S-470) and turn right (north). Continue another 0.6 miles and turn right (east) onto Barn Road. (The trail marker here has disappeared twice, so pay attention to the turn.) Follow for another 0.5 miles and turn left (north) on Pauline Drive, which you will follow until a right (east) turn onto General Moultrie Road. This will take you back to the Lake Moultrie dike system. Be sure to watch for

A railroad trestle allows visitors to cross over the Old Santee Canal on the Palmetto Trail's Lake Moultrie Passage.

trail markers along the road.

Once the trail re-joins the dike system, it remains here — with brief exceptions — for approximately the next 13.8 miles. Constructed by Santee Cooper, the dike is entirely earthen. On the lake side you'll see many bald cypress, water lilies and other flora in the marshy patches and bays. Turtles and waterfowl are common, and during one trip we saw a massive alligator at least 10 feet long sunning on the banks. On the land side, the forest is a combination of pine and hardwood with countless wildflowers. The walking is enjoyable and easy.

There is a primitive campground approximately 1.8 miles after leaving the Bonneau Beach community. (You can find the campsite 0.3 miles off the trail, between the dike and water. The road here is a dirt extension of Berkeley County S-41.)

After 3.9 miles, the trail reaches a boat landing at the Rediversion Canal near Russellville. The trail markers are sometimes hard to follow here. Take the Russellville Spur trail for easy access to the Old Store and Museum. Until then, follow the paved road (Berkeley County S-204) approximately 1.25 miles back out to

Berkeley County S-35. Turn right and walk approximately 100 yards to find the store.

At the Rediversion Canal, you will follow a gravel road adjacent to the canal inland (northeast) for one mile where you may cross at the next bridge, which is Berkeley County S-35. **This detour is not well marked! Continue straight across a grassy patch where the trail veers left and underneath Hwy. 35. Use extreme caution when crossing the bridge at Hwy. 35. On the other side turn left near the parking lot for the Canal WMA and follow another gravel road back southwest along the canal. This two-mile detour is necessary because there are no other canal crossings available.

Once you re-join the dike system, follow for another 3.6 miles to a campsite and one of the best areas along the trail. This is the beginning of Sandy Beach Wildlife Management Area (WMA). The Sandy Beach Trail (which is only open from March 2 to Nov. 15) follows a series of WMA access roads deep into this prime waterfowl habitat. Budget some time to enjoy 6.2 miles of trails here where you'll find excellent views of the lake, many ducks, migrating birds and even a bald eagle.

Mountain biking is a popular sport on the Palmetto Trail. The great variety in trail conditions offers a real challenge with about as many bikers as hikers using the trail.

There are also two, highly recommended primitive campsites in the Sandy Beach area, including one 0.2 miles from the main trail and inside the main dike.

The main Lake Moultrie Passage continues northwest along the dike 2.5 miles after the campsite sign until it dead-ends at Old Santee Canal. Here, you'll cross on a railroad trestle and continue another 0.5 mile into a dense stand of hardwoods and pine. This portion of the trail is enjoyably dark and swampy, since solid boardwalks allow you passage over the deep bogs and Quattlebaum's Canal. In wet weather they are slick, though, so mountain bikers will want to make sure they don't slide off the boardwalks!

The final five miles of trail dart in and out of marshy woodlands, crosses railroad tracks and several county roads to an unpaved road where there is a large campsite with hand-pump and water. This path continues another 1.5 miles to the Diversion Canal, where you'll skirt huge mounds of kudzu-covered dirt to reach the parking area. The final portion of trail is undignified and somewhat ugly.

People & Places

Old Store and Museum
The quirkiest little store (close to the PT)

1721 Hwy. 35, P.O. Box 23, Russellville, SC 29476, (843) 567-2255.

As a native Lowcountry girl — and one-time Californian — Teddy Kieley doesn't see things the same way others do in her tiny community of Russellville.

When the Palmetto Trail began becoming a reality, she didn't wonder why people would want to hike along Lake Moultrie.

She hatched plans to build a spur trail off the Lake Moultrie Passage that would lead to her shop, the Old Store and Museum. She started converting a back room into museum space and

Teddy Kieley owns the Old Store and Museum, which is open seven days a week. The store is just a short way off the Palmetto Trail in Russellville.

even dreams of opening an inn just for tired hikers. Kieley also leads a small citizens' advocacy group, the Swamp Fox Conservancy, which wrestles with environmental and historical issues. In other words, she likes to think of the Old Store and Museum as more than just a way station not far from the Palmetto Trail.

Kieley bought the Old Store and Museum (locals also call it the Old Russellville Store and the Harold Crawford Store after its previous owner) in 1996. She sells seed, groceries, fishing supplies and plenty of candy for the local kids. Make sure Kieley takes you into the back room where you can peruse decades-old farming relics such as drills, hand-made pulleys and kitchen utensils.

But the real treat here is Kieley herself, who's around seven days a week. About the only time you won't find her is between 11 and noon on Sundays. "This town shuts down so we can all go to church together," she said. "Russellville has that small-town feel, alright." Take a few minutes to talk with Teddy about additional recreational opportunities around Russellville.

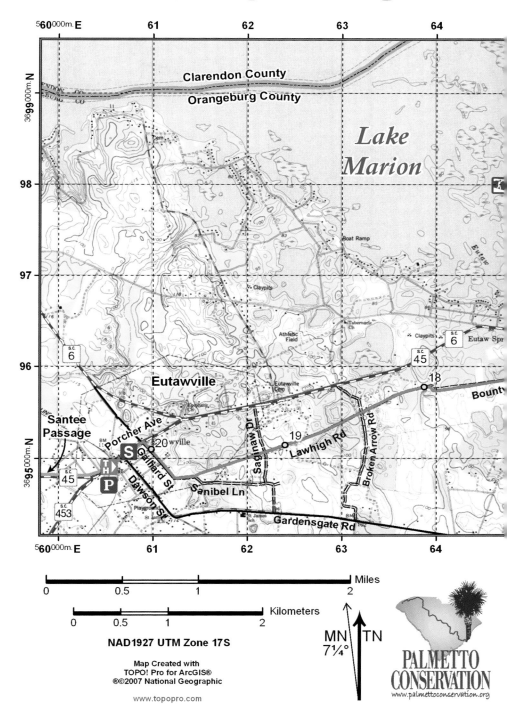

Clarendon County
Orangeburg County

Lake Marion

Boat Ramp

Claypits

Tabernacle Ch.

Athletic Field

Claypits

Eutaw Spr

Eutawville

Eutawville Cem

Bounty

Santee Passage

Porcher Ave

wville

Saginaw Dr

Lawhigh Rd

Broken Arrow Rd

Gaillard St

Dawson St

Sanibel Ln

St. James Sch

Gardensgate Rd

Playgd

S.C. 6

S.C. 45

S.C. 6

S.C. 45

S.C. 453

18

19

20

Miles
0   0.5   1   2

Kilometers
0   0.5   1   2

NAD1927 UTM Zone 17S

Map Created with
TOPO! Pro for ArcGIS®
®©2007 National Geographic

www.topopro.com

MN
7¼°   TN

PALMETTO
CONSERVATION
www.palmettoconservation.org

almetto Trail - Section 1

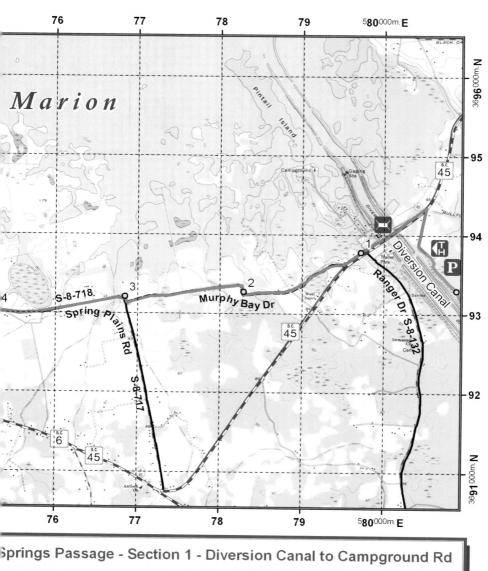

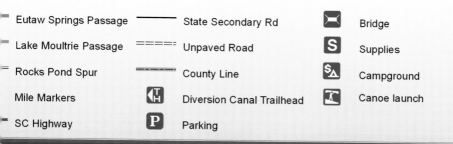

Springs Passage - Section 1 - Diversion Canal to Campground Rd

Eutaw Springs Passage	State Secondary Rd	⊠	Bridge
Lake Moultrie Passage	Unpaved Road	S	Supplies
Rocks Pond Spur	County Line	S⚊	Campground
Mile Markers	Diversion Canal Trailhead	⛆	Canoe launch
SC Highway	Parking		

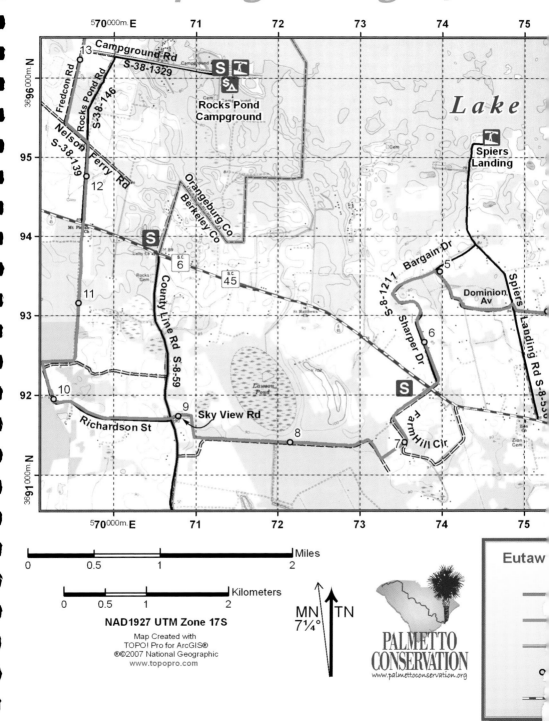

570000m. E   71   72   73   74   75

Campground Rd
S-38-1329
13
Rocks Pond
Campground
Fredcon Rd
Rocks Pond Rd
S-38-146
Nelson Ferry Rd
S-38-139
12
Orangeburg Co
Berkeley Co
S.C. 6
S.C. 45
County Line Rd S-8-59
11
10
Richardson St
9
Sky View Rd
8
Spiers Landing
Bargain Dr
5
Dominion Av
S-8-1211
Sharper Dr
6
Farm Hill Cir
7
Spiers Landing Rd S-8-330

396000m. N
95
94
93
92
3691000m. N

Miles
0   0.5   1   2

Kilometers
0   0.5   1   2

NAD1927 UTM Zone 17S

Map Created with
TOPO! Pro for ArcGIS®
®©2007 National Geographic
www.topopro.com

MN
7¼°
TN

**PALMETTO
CONSERVATION**
www.palmettoconservation.org

Eutaw

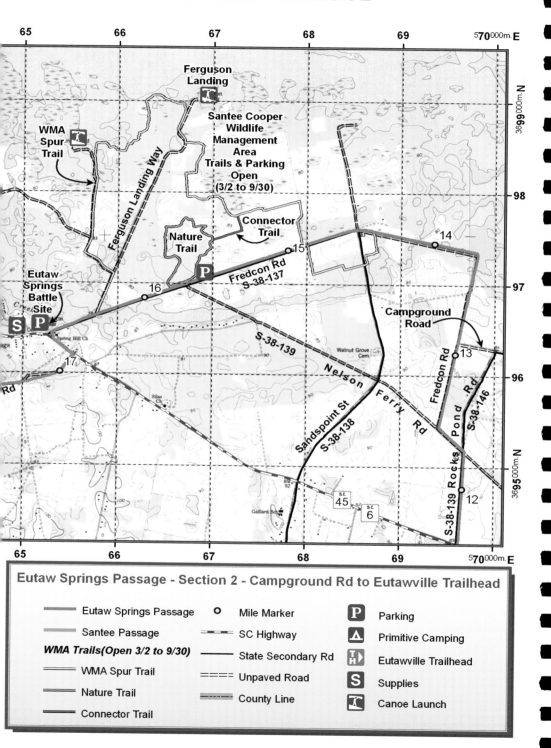

Eutaw Springs Passage - Section 2 - Campground Rd to Eutawville Trailhead

▬▬▬ Eutaw Springs Passage	○ Mile Marker	**P** Parking	
▬▬▬ Santee Passage	▬ ▪ ▬ SC Highway	▲ Primitive Camping	
WMA Trails(Open 3/2 to 9/30)	▬ State Secondary Rd	**TH** Eutawville Trailhead	
▬ WMA Spur Trail	==== Unpaved Road	**S** Supplies	
▬▬▬ Nature Trail	▬▬▬ County Line	Canoe Launch	
▬▬▬ Connector Trail			

Eutaw Springs Passage

M ore than a simple connector trail between Orangeburg and Berkeley counties, the Eutaw Springs Passage of the Palmetto Trail pushes through a varied terrain of grassy pastures, tiny downtown Eutawville and shady dirt roads.

It's an enjoyable slice of Lowcountry South Carolina — complete with nearby access to world-class barbecue, Revolutionary War historical sites, and carnival style RV campgrounds. The southern portion of the trail follows rural dirt roads through some unremarkable terrain. Some trail users prefer to travel west along SC Hwy 6 while others prefer the solitude of a woods trail.

But the best part of this trail comes closer to Eutawville where you'll travel through old pasture fields once part of a dairy farm. The spur trail is closed periodically on Saturday mornings for youth game hunts. Signs will indicate closure and you must use the Palmetto Trail route during those times. The trail ends at Eutawville Town Hall, which isn't far from trinket shops and lots of friendly people.

Difficulty: Easy if done in sections as a day hike, moderate otherwise

Length: 20 miles. Spur trails add approximately 5 miles

Fees: None

Conditions: Generally good. Much of this trail uses rural highways and dirt roads. You should prepare for possibility of unleashed dogs and wear bright clothing (and reflectors) to warn drivers. The spur trail is occasionally wet and muddy.

USGS Quadrangles: Pineville, Eutawville

Directions: *For the southern trailhead:* From Pineville, drive six miles on SC 45 past the turn at Sandy Beach Road. Just before a bridge, turn left onto Eadie Lane

On the Eutaw Springs Passage, pine woods surround rural, dirt roads which makes for enjoyable exploring.

at trailhead sign on SC 45. Follow the dirt road past homes on the left for 0.4 miles to the second pullout on the right (don't park in the cul-de-sac with a fire ring overlooking the canal). Instead, look for small, yellow trail markers at a stand of pine trees and adjacent to a fenced-in lot of quarried rock. Park here. The Lake Moultrie Passage ends here; to begin the Eutaw Springs Passage, backtrack to SC 45, cross the Diversion Canal on the bridge *(the pedestrian lane on the new bridge offers the user a safe passage)* and continue west on SC 45 for 0.25 miles. Turn right onto Murphy Bay Road.

For the Eutaw Springs Battleground trailhead: From Eutawville, continue four miles on SC 45 to where the road splits. Veer left as if onto Fredcon Drive and park on the left at a parking area.

For the northern trailhead: The northern trailhead is located at the Eutawville Town Hall on SC 45.

Hours: Year-round

Camping: Primitive backcountry camping

is available in the dairy farm property off Battlefield Drive (no water). Numerous tent sites and RV-style camping are available at Rocks Pond Campground.

Information: Contact Palmetto Conservation, 1314 Lincoln St., Suite 305, Columbia, S.C. 29201-3154 (803) 771-0870

On the Trail

From the trailhead at the Diversion Canal, backtrack 0.4 miles out to SC 45 and turn left (west). Cross the bridge *(use the pedestrian lane on the new SC 45 bridge over the diversion canal)* and continue down SC 45 for another 0.25-mile to a right turn at Murphy Bay Road (dirt). For the next five miles, the trail follows dirt and paved roads through a rural residential area. Follow Murphy Bay to a right turn onto paved Spring Plains Road and continue to a left turn at Dominion Road, which is dirt. Follow this to a left turn at paved Bargain Drive;

Rural, dirt roads provide fast routes for mountain bikers on portions of the Eutaw Springs Passage.

continue to another left onto Sharper Road (also paved), which you will follow to SC 6/45 near Pete's Quick Stop. You can find re-supplies inside if needed.

The trail continues straight across SC 6/45 on Sharper Road (which is dirt) and veers off the dirt road, between some small fields and into gorgeous, dense pine woodland. The trail then follows a seldom used woods road through a thick pine with a dense canopy. At the pipe gate continue straight as the road bears left. A sharp right will take you to a dirt path and left out to a paved road. Continue straight across and along a paved road and just after the paved road turns right (the road becomes dirt again here) the trail will parallel the road (on the left) just insides the woods along a deep ditch. A right turn will follow an old fire break, turning left and continue out to SC 6/45. This is a really nice section of trail with open sight distance along the trail to spot wildlife crossing your path. You are now on Rocks Pond Road (paved) and at a Y-shaped intersection, veer left onto Nelson Ferry Road (dirt) and then make a quick right onto Fredcon Road. Follow this dirt road to when it cuts left and eventually emerges at a four-way stop.

You have two options here. If you are hiking between March 2 and September 30, you can turn left (south) onto a spur trail with white blazes. At any other time, continue straight on Fredcon Road to the Eutaw Springs Battlefield site on the right.

The spur trail is an enjoyable and highly recommended diversion. The initial portion continues south into a game field and then west through open corridors between stands of pine and game fields. Cross two roads, including Fredcon again, and continue straight into another woodland. Here, it skirts a field of corn, sunflowers, pea and winter wheat maintained by the S.C. Dept. of Natural Resources. Keep your eyes open, because

Much of the Palmetto Trail is on private land and many landowners do regular maintenance on the trail. Remember to respect private property and stay on the trail.

there is a Y-shaped break in the trail soon; the right path continues on the spur trail, left leads to a two-mile loop through Santee Cooper Wildlife Management Area Nature Trail.

This nature trail is an enjoyable, flat path through a mixed hardwood forest with many young pines, sweetgum, hickory and small oak. Along the way you may see nesting boxes for wildlife, especially kestrel or "sparrow hawk" and bluebirds. Many birds make their home in this small section of trail including red-eyed vireo, Acadian flycatcher, ruby-crowned kinglet, loggerhead shrike, indigo bunting and the rufous-sided towhee. Other points of interest include a limestone sink pond and wooden bridge over old Nelson's Ferry

Road, which was an important trade route between North Carolina and Charleston in the late 1700s and early 1800s.

By staying right on the spur trail, you will soon cut left onto Ferguson Landing Way and follow this dirt road under a canopy of oak and cypress around Snug's Curve to Miller's Landing. Here, the trail dives back into the pine trees again, following white blazes through tall broomsedge grass.

The trail continues another 1.1 miles through relatively obvious ground to a large, grassy clearing. The ground is often wet and soft here, but you should skirt the field to the right (northeast) and find an open path. White-tailed deer are very common here, even midday. Before long, white blazes resume again on the left and you will continue until you emerge at a dirt road. Bear left here and continue on this dirt road for approximately 1.5 miles past cornfields to a DNR Agricultural Station and kiosk for dove hunters. Drinkable well water is available from a hand pump here.

Stay on the dirt road until it ends at Ferguson Landing Way, where you will turn right (south) and follow to Fredcon Road. Fredcon continues past the Eutaw

The spur trail on the Eutaw Springs Passage will allow you to get some excellent views of Lake Marion.

Occasionally, landowners will do controlled burns in the Lowcountry. After one such burn on the former dairy farm property, the Palmetto Trail has a surreal, moonscape look to it as a mountain biker rides past a trail post.

Springs Battle Site and then turns left onto SC 6/45. Follow 300 yards to a right turn at Battlefield Drive. Stay on Battlefield

Drive until the road begins to curve left and look on the right for trail blazes. Follow into the woods past Palmetto Trail signs and into a large field. This land was once a dairy farm and you'll see remnants of an old grain barn along the way. Please stay on the trail here since this land is private property.

The next few miles are among the trail's best. Warblers and vireo inhabit the sassafras, loblolly and chinquapin trees around here. The trail continues through the dairy farm land until it deposits you onto a dirt county road.

Continue here past one especially ugly dumping area and re-emerge at a residential neighborhood, where you will follow blazes back to SC 6/45 and downtown Eutawville. The trailhead is Town Hall.

People & Places

Rock's Pond Campground
A camping carnival.

108 Campground Road
Eutawville, SC 29048, (803) 492-7711, (800) 982-0271 outside SC.

Rutledge Connor takes a nap in late morning and again in early afternoon. But if you catch him any other time, Rut — as everybody around here calls him — usually puts on quite a

Rut Connor owns the huge Rock's Pond Campground, which is just a short detour off the Palmetto Trail.

show. One of his staff swears Connor is the only person who lives as though the Civil War hasn't ended yet and actually gets away with it.

Connor owns the huge Rock's Pond Campground and Marina on Rock's Pond Road, just a short detour off the Eutaw Springs Passage. The family-oriented campground caters primarily to the RV and sport fishing crowd. In other words, hard-core backpackers won't find much fireside solitude.

Instead, it's the type of layover where you could spend rest days fishing off the pier, shooting skeet, swimming in a pool or exploring the eponymously named Mount Rutmore (ask when you get there).

Although the campground literally teems with people during warm weather holidays — sometimes making it difficult to find a space — things can be downright relaxing during cool weather. Connor opened the campsite in 1964 on a site once used for shipbuilding in the 1790s and early 1800s.

If you run into him exploring the grounds, don't feel put-off by his cantankerous demeanor. Stick around long enough and he'll start offering all kinds of stories.

"I'm an admirer of the American way," he says, waving his hand at the campground behind him, parts of which he leases from Santee Cooper. "People around here think I'm crazy as hell… but it's not so. I just had an idea of what I wanted to do here and I did it.

"We do it all here and that's why people come from all over to see us."

Sweatman's Bar-b-que
One argument for 'scheduling' your trip.

Hwy. 453, Holly Hill, SC, No phone.

Although it's only open on Fridays and Saturdays, Sweatman's Bar-b-que on SC 453 is the kind of place you would consider taking a six-mile detour to visit.

It's even the kind of place you would consider re-arranging trip plans so you could drop by during its two open days during the week. Because if you're a fan of Southern pork barbecue, this is one joint on the Lowcountry section of the Palmetto Trail you won't want to miss.

Although it's only open on Friday and Saturday, a visit to Sweatman's Bar-b-que is good reason to schedule trips for the weekend on the Eutaw Springs Passage of the Palmetto Trail.

Outside, Sweatman's has all the markings of a genuine barbecue hut. A covered porch surrounds the front and an aluminum roof glares in the hot Lowcountry sun. A little pink pig greets you on the walkway up to the take-out side and if you drop by during an off day you might be able to smell the pork cooking slowly out back.

Once inside, people just pretty much shuffle toward the buffet room. Unlike most barbecue places, you're only allowed one trip down the line here. (First-timers get seconds... but don't try to pass as one. They'll sniff you out!) Instead, the key is using two paper plates for a sturdy plate so you can pile on more barbecue than is probably healthy.

In town, they'll tell you Sweatman's does both red and yellow-style barbecue. That's just a Southern way of saying they do both mustard and ketchup-based sauce. The buffet line includes all the usuals: veggies, rolls and iced tea. It's simple. But Sweatman's is a regional landmark for a reason...

Hours: 11:30 a.m. to 9:30 p.m. in the summer (just 9 p.m. in the winter)

Price range: $4 to $6 per plate.

How to pay: Cash. (No credit cards or checks.)

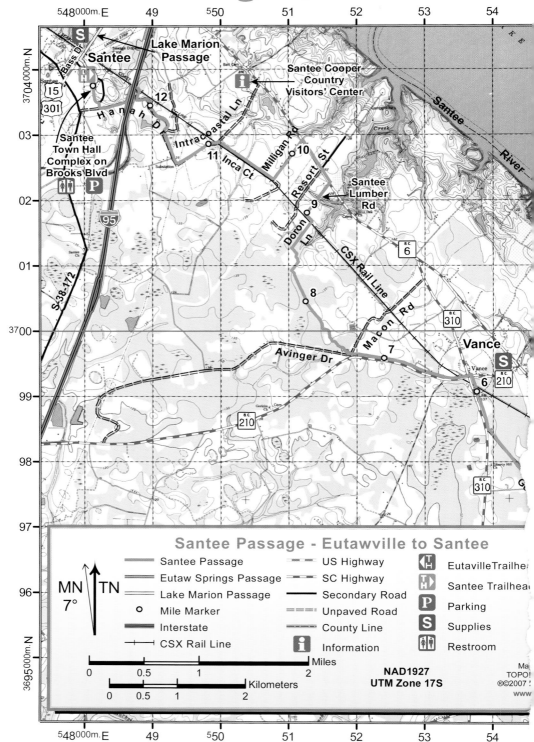

Santee Passage - Eutawville to Santee

Legend:
- Santee Passage
- Eutaw Springs Passage
- Lake Marion Passage
- Mile Marker ○
- Interstate
- CSX Rail Line
- US Highway
- SC Highway
- Secondary Road
- Unpaved Road
- County Line
- Information **i**
- Eutaville Trailhead
- Santee Trailhead
- Parking **P**
- Supplies **S**
- Restroom

MN / TN 7°

Miles
0 0.5 1 2

Kilometers
0 0.5 1 2

NAD1927
UTM Zone 17S

Map labels: Lake Marion Passage, Santee, Santee Cooper Country Visitors' Center, Intracoastal Ln, Santee Town Hall Complex on Brooks Blvd, Milligan Rd, Resort St, Santee Lumber Rd, Inca Ct, Doron Ln, CSX Rail Line, Macon Rd, Avinger Dr, Vance, Hanah Dr, Bass Dr, Santee River

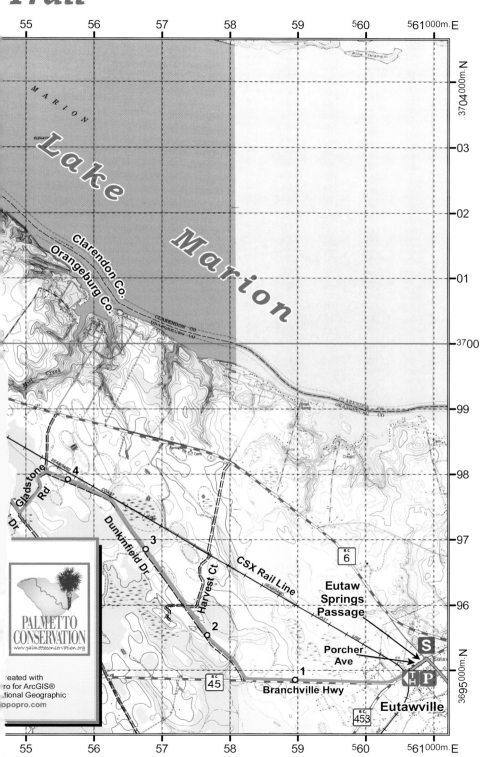

55   56   57   58   59   560   561 000m.E

3704000m.N
03
02
01
3700
99
98
97
96
3695000m.N

MARION

Lake Marion

ELEVAT

Clarendon Co.
Orangeburg Co.
CLARENDON CO.
ORANGEBURG CO.

Pine Island

Gladstone Rd
Dr
Dr

Dunkinfield Dr

Harvest Ct

CSX Rail Line

SEABOARD COAST LINE

SC 6

Eutaw
Springs
Passage

Porcher
Ave

4
3
2
1

SC 45

Branchville Hwy

SC 453

Eutawville

S

H P

PALMETTO
CONSERVATION
www.palmettoconservation.org

reated with
ro for ArcGIS®
tional Geographic
opopro.com

55   56   57   58   59   560   561 000m.E

Santee Passage

L ots of dirt roads and time on rural highways make this a pleasant trip for mountain bikers. However, hikers may have to spend more time in "civilization" than we usually prefer. The 13-mile passage winds through the predominantly agricultural lands of eastern Orangeburg County and uses many "farm-to-market" roads. Meanwhile, the adjacent lands present a tapestry of color and texture with a variety of crops such as cotton, wheat, soybeans and canola. Nearby produce stands offer seasonal delights including fresh strawberries, blueberries and peaches.

The pot of gold on this trail is the shady portion across land owned by Mona and the late Ira Avinger. Take time to enjoy your time in the pine woods and beneath some whopping oak trees.

This passage eventually crosses under bustling Interstate 95 on dirt roads and emerges at the tourist town of Santee, the official "Gateway to the Lowcountry" for the Palmetto Trail.

Difficulty: Easy

Length: 13 miles

Fees: None

Conditions: Much of this trail uses rural highways and dirt roads. You should prepare for possibility of unleashed dogs and wear bright clothing (and reflectors) to warn drivers. High temperatures and biting insects (mosquitoes, chiggers and ticks) can be a problem in warm weather.

USGS Quadrangles: Vance, Eutawville

Directions: *For the northern trailhead:* From Columbia or Charleston, follow Interstate 26 to Interstate 95 where you will continue north. Santee is exit 98. US 301/15 runs directly through the middle of town; turn at the Fire House/EMS Station and proceed to the Santee Cultural Arts and Visitors Center.

For the southern trailhead: The southern trailhead is located at the Eutawville Town Hall on SC 45.

Hours: Year-round

Some sections the Palmetto Trail near Santee traverse fields dotted with massive oak trees.

*Wildlife food plots and agricultural fields offer a plentiful supply of food for wild game.
These fields and plots of frequently visited by deer, turkey and a number of songbirds.
Small animals find refuge and cover for protection as well as plenty of grain to eat.*

Camping: None on the trail. Nearby camping is available at Santee State Park.

Information: Contact Palmetto Conservation, 1314 Lincoln St., Suite 305, Columbia, S.C. 29201-3154. (803) 771-0870.

On the Trail

From the trailhead at Eutawville Town Hall, follow SC 45 through town and continue west for approximately 1.5-miles to a right (north) turn at Dukenfield Drive. Continue to a three-way intersection where you will veer left (southwest) onto Gladstone Road. Continue on Gladstone Road until it dead-ends at another dirt road, Gemini Drive. Large trucks frequent Gemini Road on their way to nearby industrial sites, so hikers and bikers should

also pay close attention at curves or during times of low visibility. Follow Gemini Drive to an intersection with SC 310, where you will bear right and continue into the tiny town of Vance. Here, turn left onto SC 210 and follow approximately one mile to a church and cemetery on the right. The Palmetto Trail dives into the woods behind the church, although it is well marked and obvious.

This is the best section of trail on this passage. Here, the woods close in around you and the trail squeezes tightly through some narrow passages recently cleared by Palmetto Trail workers, volunteers and AmeriCorps crews. Downed trees may still pose an occasional obstacle in this newly cut passage, but surmounting them is usually straightforward. The trail continues directly through one open field, along an irrigation ditch and past some farmland and gigantic oak trees. Eventually, the trail emerges at a large farmland and continues right (north) along a dirt road. The road crosses over the railroad and continues out to SC Hwy 6. Left along the highway and the trail turns left on Milligan Rd (dirt road) and then right on Inca Ct. Use your map and check the web for changes along here as land ownership patterns change frequently. From Inca Ct. the trail uses Intracoastal Ln. on into Hannah Rd. This dirt road winds around several curves and under Interstate 95 to the backside of the Santee Cultural Arts and Visitors Center in the Town Hall Complex where there is a kiosk and trailhead.

People & Places

Lowcountry life
Exploring the Avinger's property

One of the best portions of the Santee Passage runs through a dense stand of pine trees, carefully manicured farmland and some irrigation ditches so deep that trail workers had to build wooden bridges to span them. A portion of this property belongs to Mona and the late Ira Avinger, the friendly farmers whose family has lived on this land since the 1730s.

Ira Avinger was an energetic man who loved the idea of hikers and mountain bikers exploring the woods nearby.

"I've got no objection at all as long as they're decent people," he always said. "All I ask is that people don't burn the woods. I'm scared of fire."

Ira used to fly single-engine prop planes from his own landing strip and airplane hangar. Some of the property still shows the effects of Hurricane Hugo — the windmill is still mangled — but the Avingers always worked hard to make their land and the community of Vance a bright spot along the Palmetto Trail.

Mona and the late Ira Avinger allowed the Santee Passage of the Palmetto Trail to cross their wooded farmland property.

"If you want to get out there and explore the land God created, then you're my buddy," Ira used to say. "I'm all for it."

Clark's Restaurant
A Santee Institution

114 Bradford Blvd., Santee, SC 29142, (803) 854-2141, (803) 854-2004 fax, (800) 531-9658 reservations.

Way back in 1946 — locals like to say — William E. Clark saw the future.

Having just returned from World War II and started his own family, Clark was looking for something to do with his life. But with few family assets and unwilling to commit his life to farming, Clark opted to take a chance in the tiny crossroads town of Santee. Although the town then had just three stores, a bus station and a post office, Clark thought Santee might eventually grow because it was located on US 301 — then the primary route between New York and Florida. He guessed people would soon begin traveling more and highway property might make a good investment.

So, having been a mess sergeant in the Army, Clark decided to buy the town's old bus station and turn it into a restaurant: Clark's.

In the ensuing years, the little joint grew into the town's most popular establishment with a façade that Clark's son Bill likens to the Alamo. When Interstate 95 opened in 1971, Clark moved the restaurant to its present location and added a quaint inn that still appeals to travelers.

Today, Clark's family, particularly Bill, runs the restaurant, inn and spin-off real estate business. Bill Clark has lived in Santee for all of his life and can still remember the days before I-95. He's now working to change Santee from an interstate exchange into a community.

"I think we're finally on the road now," he said from his office next door to Clark's. "We want to be more than just neon signs and hotels. With all the golf, fishing and hunting nearby this town could really be something great."

Clark's — of course — will remain at the center of it all.

With Calabash style seafood, catfish filets and fireside dining, the restaurant has long been a tradition for many Lowcountry residents. Open at 6 a.m. daily, you can order breakfast, lunch or dinner as well as golf and fishing packages. Rooms start from $45.

Clark's Inn & Restaurant has been a popular traveler's stopover in Santee since it was originally established in 1946.

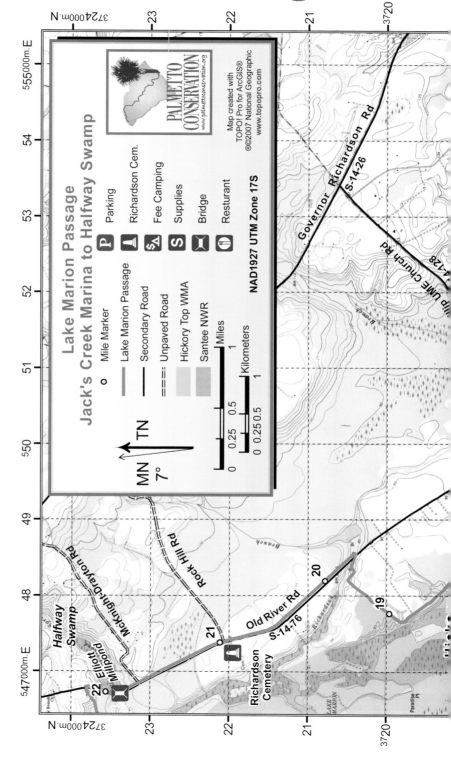

Lake Marion Passage
Jack's Creek Marina to Halfway Swamp

PALMETTO CONSERVATION
www.palmettoconservation.org

Map created with
TOPO! Pro for ArcGIS®
®©2007 National Geographic
www.topopro.com

NAD1927 UTM Zone 17S

- o Mile Marker
- — Lake Marion Passage
- — Secondary Road
- =≡= Unpaved Road
- ▒ Hickory Top WMA
- ▒ Santee NWR

- P Parking
- ⛺ Richardson Cem.
- $⛺ Fee Camping
- S Supplies
- X Bridge
- ⊕ Resturant

MN
7°
TN

Miles
0   0.25   0.5   1
0 0.25 0.5   1
Kilometers

Governor Richardson Rd
S-14-26
14-128
UME Church Rd
Branch
Rock Hill Rd
McKnight-Dayton Rd
Halfway Swamp
Elliott Millpond
Richardson Cemetery
Old River Rd
S-14-76
Richardson
Branch
LAKE MARION
Paradise Pt

22
21
20
19
23
22
21
3720

555000m.E   554   553   552   551   550   549   548   547000m.E

3724000m.N   23   22   21   3720

3724000m.N

Palmetto Trail - Section 2

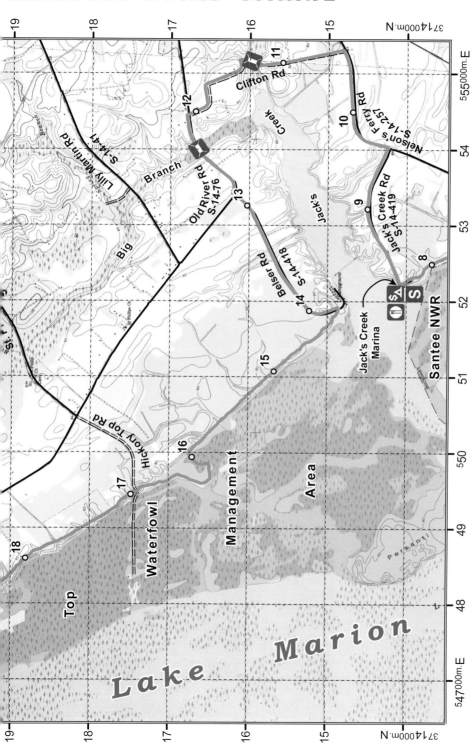

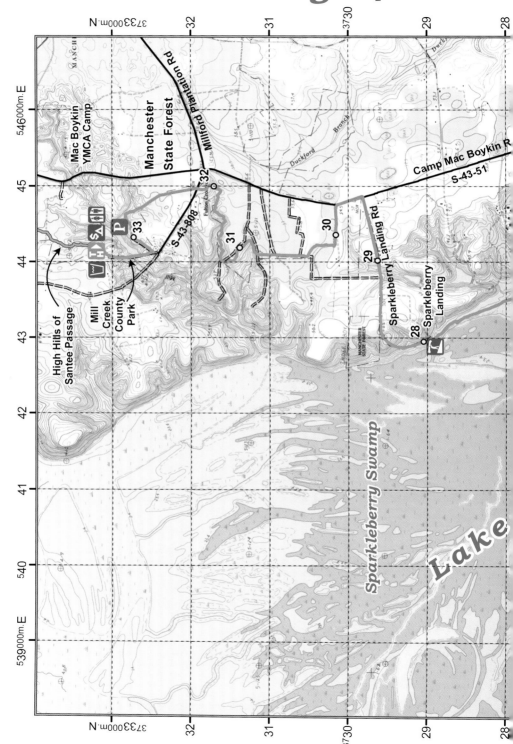

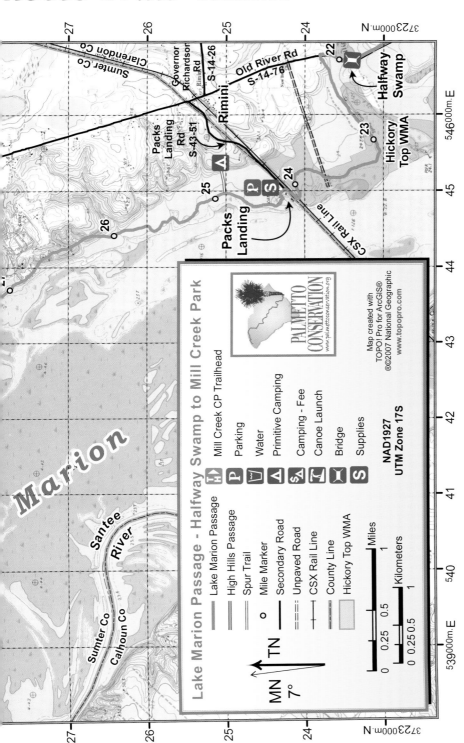

Lake Marion Passage - Halfway Swamp to Mill Creek Park

PALMETTO CONSERVATION
www.palmettoconservation.org

Map created with
TOPO! Pro for ArcGIS®
©©2007 National Geographic
www.topo.pro.com

NAD1927
UTM Zone 17S

Lake Marion Passage
High Hills Passage
Spur Trail
o Mile Marker
Secondary Road
Unpaved Road
CSX Rail Line
County Line
Hickory Top WMA

Mill Creek CP Trailhead
Parking
Water
Primitive Camping
Camping - Fee
Canoe Launch
Bridge
Supplies

MN TN
7°

0   0.25   0.5   1   Miles
0 0.25 0.5   1   Kilometers

Marion

Santee River

Sumter Co
Calhoun Co

Packs Landing

Packs Landing Rd
S-43-51

Rimini

Sumter Co
Clarendon Co

Governor Richardson Rd
Rimini Rd
S-14-26

Old River Rd
S-14-76

Halfway Swamp

Hickory Top WMA

CSX Rail Line

22
23
24
25
26

539000m. E
540
41
42
43
44
45
546000m. E

3723000m. N
27   26   25   24

Lake Marion Passage

This 33 mile passage of the Palmetto Trail skirts along the high water mark of the north side of Lake Marion. Trail users will enjoy some of the most magnificent vistas in the coastal plain with opportunities to spot abundant wildlife and colorful flora. Deer, turkey, squirrels, fox and waterfowl are numerous. Users should plan for the possibility of encountering poisonous snakes and large alligators along the lake's edge. An occasional otter may be spotted playing in the shallow waters of the lake.

Only hikers and bikers may use this section of trail. The Lake Marion Passage is marked with orange blazes from Mill Creek County Park to Sparkleberry Landing with the remainder being marked by yellow blazes. Much of the land along the trail is open for hunting and users should wear bright colors during big game hunting seasons, which is from the middle of August to January.

Because of the trail's proximity to Lake Marion some sections may be flooded during the wet season. However, these wet conditions add to the beauty of the area with a profusion of wildflowers. Almost year-round the pink, yellow, and blue colors will thrill you with their beauty.

Difficulty: Moderate

Length: 33 miles

Fees: None

Conditions: Much of the trail is in very remote locations, only occasionally emerging at a boat landing. June through September is the wet season and water can soak the ground along the trail tread. Lake levels can cause flooding of the trail tread. High temperatures and high humidity can be a problem during the summer months. Insects along this passage are a real problem – ticks, chiggers, mosquitoes. Biting flies are numerous beginning in late May through September. Snakes and alligators call the

The Lake Marion Passage skirts along the north side of Lake Marion and offers magnificent vistas of the lake and the wildlife. Winter brings an abundance of waterfowl.

ecosystem home, including the venomous snake varieties. Alligators are especially large but are just as afraid of you as you are of them. Potable water is available at a number of locations along the trail and is shown on the map.

USGS Quadrangles: Lone Star, Pinewood, St. Paul and Vance

Directions: *For the Santee Town Hall Complex trailhead:* From Columbia or Charleston, follow I-26 to I-95, north on I-95 to exit 98, turn left on SC 6, then turn left at the stop light on US 301. Drive south for one mile, turn left at Fire House to park at Town Hall.

For Pack's Landing: Turn to the west at Rimini (the Sumter/Clarendon County line) off of Camp Mac Boykin Road and proceed 1.4 miles to parking.

For Mill Creek County Park: From the junction of US 378 and SC 261 travel 12.5 miles south to Camp Mac Boykin Road. Take right-hand fork (sign says to Rimini), travel 3 miles and turn right on Milford Plantation Road, travel .8 miles to Mill Creek County Park. Parking is allowed in the day-use area.

Hours: Year-round. Night hiking permitted

Camping: Arbuckle's Landing is a commercial campground just off Scotts Lake Road on the north side of Lake Marion. Call them at (803) 478-5269 for tent camping sites or just drop-in.

Jacks Creek Marina offers commercial tent camping sites overlooking the lake. These are really nice sites and you can contact them at (803) 478-2793.

About a quarter mile past Packs Landing and off to the right there is a primitive camp site on high ground. It's a couple hundred yards over to the site and the trail over can be wet with standing water after rains.

Camping is permitted at **Mill Creek County Park** but you need to make

Mill Creek County Park at the northern end of the Lake Marion Passage offers camping with bathrooms and showers.

arrangements in advance. Contact the park management at Mill Creek County Park, 7975 Millford Plantation Road, Pinewood, SC 29125, (803) 436-2248

Information: Contact Manchester State Forest, 7640 Headquarters Road, Wedgefield, SC 29168, (803) 494-8196

Mill Creek County Park, 7975 Millford Plantation Road, Pinewood, SC 29125, (803) 436-2248

Santee Cooper Land Division, One Riverwood Drive, Moncks Corner, SC 29461, (843) 761-8000

Santee National Wildlife Refuge, 2125 Ft Watson Rd., Summerton, SC 29148, (803) 478-2217

Palmetto Conservation, 1314 Lincoln Street, Suite 305, Columbia, SC 29201-3154, (803) 771-0870

On The Trail

The trail leaves the Santee Town Hall Complex with an information board at the Santee Cultural Arts & Visitors Center on Brooks Drive. Take a right at Bass Drive

(Old US Hwy 301) and follow the sidewalk north. The trail utilizes the abandoned US 301 causeway over Lake Marion.

Arbuckle's landing off Scotts Lake Road on the north side of Lake Marion offers tent camping sites in a commercial campground. You can call the campground at (803) 478-5269 for more information.

The E-Z Shop on the left has a complete line of supplies from fresh doughnuts to fishing bait. You will find it a convenient place to stop right on the trail. Just past the shop the Ft. Watson Road turns to the left and leads to the Santee National Wildlife Refuge Headquarters and the Santee Indian Mound plus a really nice nature trail. A stop here would be worth your time.

A little over a mile from the lake the trail turns left on Nelson Ferry Road. After about a quarter mile you can duck into the woods between the road and the lake or continue along the road past several vacation homes on the left, and then just past the last home, duck back into the woods.

You are now on the Santee National Wildlife Refuge. They have some regulations that don't apply on other lands. They are simple but are enforced: no firearms, no dogs, no night hiking, no camping, and no parking on the refuge. Other than these the rule is simple: just enjoy one of the nicest sections along the trail.

The trail parallels Cantey Bay on Lake Marion. The bay fills with waterfowl during the winter months and the sound of ducks, geese and other waterfowl fill the air. You often get frequent glimpses of the birds out on the water. The forest is young pines planted in old agricultural fields and large oaks on the high ground along the lake. Just before Jacks Creek there is a community of dwarf palmettos. South Carolina has two palmetto species. We are all familiar with the palmetto tree which is the state tree but the other species is dwarf

DETOURS

The Santee Indian Mound & Ft. Watson

At the end of Ft. Watson Road stands a large hill on the north shore of Lake Marion. Known as the Santee Indian Mound, it was part of an Indian culture that flourished over 3,000 years ago. The Santee Indians were part of the Mississippi culture and used the mound for ceremonial and burial purposes. Most likely a village surrounded the mound which is the only ceremonial center ever located in the coastal plain.

By the beginning of the American Revolution, the site had been abandoned by the Indians. The site, however, took on a new and more violent role during this period.

During the American Revolution the British established a fort here to control movement on the Santee River as well as the main road between Charleston and Camden. It was a strategic location and the mound was used as a part of their fortifications.

On April 15, 1871, General Francis Marion and Lt. Col. Henry "Lighthorse Harry" Lee encircled the fort and after 8 days of futile small arms fire decided a new approach was needed if they were to be successful against the British. Major Hezekiah Maham, under the cover of darkness, constructed a pine log tower of sufficient height to overlook the British stockade. Early on the morning of April 23, 1781 the Americans mounted an attack from the tower and from the ground which lasted only a short time. The British surrendered the fort, its garrison and supplies to General Francis Marion, the "Swamp Fox."

palmetto and never develops a stem.

Jacks Creek Marina offers commercial tent camping sites overlooking the lake. These are really nice sites and you can contact them at (803) 478-2793. You might ask if it is possible to catch a ferry ride over to Carolina King Retreat and Marina. No guarantees but if some of the fishing guides are available the boat ride is far superior to the hike around to the other side.

Negotiations are underway for rights-of-way to cross Jacks Creek but until then the trail makes a seven mile detour around. Use your map here as it will help tremendously. Follow Jacks Creek Road out to the left on Nelson Ferry Road and then left on Clifton Road (dirt). Clifton Road takes you through a settlement on the creek and the dogs run free. At Old River Road (paved) turn left and then left again on Belser Road. Just before entering Carolina King Retreat and Marina (formerly Billups) the trail darts sharply into the woods on the right. Tent camping isn't permitted here but the store offers drinks and snacks and cabins can be rented.

As the trail heads north it follows

The wild and remote landscape of the trail along Lake Marion was ideal for illicit activities. Moonshine whiskey was manufactured and shipped throughout the east. Today the remains of the stills can be seen in the rusty barrels along the trail.

the high water mark along Lake Marion. Flooding is possible if the water level in the lake is high and frequent rains flood the intermittent streams flowing off the adjacent land. During the wet season hikers should pick their way along on tussocks and mounds.

These forests are part of the Santee Cooper lands acquired for the hydroelectric and navigation project of the 1930's. They are wild and magnificent with large trees and dense undergrowth. There hasn't been any timber harvesting or forest management for over 60 years. A short distance in you will notice on the left a number of old rusty barrels. They are the remains of a "moonshine still" that was destroyed by the revenuers. The wild and remote nature of the woods were ideal for the illegal production of corn whiskey even up until recent times.

A little over a mile in, the trail enters a cane thicket that except for periods of drought will have standing water. As the trail leaves the thicket it passes through a willow oak flat. The understory is open and the oaks produce copious amounts of acorns. The wildlife feed off the acorns, fattening deer, squirrel and turkey. The wild azalea form mounds of underbrush and in the spring are covered with their pink flowers.

The trail passes the Hickory Top Waterfowl Management Area and follows a dirt road out to the Old River Road. During Colonial days the Old River Road would have been the travel route for the American troops retreating to the High Hills of the Santee for rest and re-supply. Looming in the distance are the white silhouettes of the stone monuments in the Richardson Cemetery. Take time to look around the cemetery.

The trail continues along the Old River Road to Halfway Swamp. The stream has been impounded and a mill pond holds

Richardson Cemetery

From some distance away as you travel the Old River Road just south of Rimini you will notice a number of bright white monuments on the horizon. They are the grave markers of Richardson descendants. Big Home Plantation would have been the ancestral home of the Richardson family, one of South Carolina's most influential families. The mansion house was built by General Richard Richardson in 1735. The location of the mansion is now lost. According to customs of the time the cemetery would have been in close proximity to the plantation house. The Richardson graveyard is one of the oldest in St. Marks Parish.

The area along the River Road was a hotbed of activity during the American Revolution. The Americans often passed the plantation as they retreated north to the High Hills of the Santee for rest and to re-supply. The British pursued the Americans only a short distance north of the Richardson estate for fear of being attacked or captured by the American sympathizers.

During the Revolutionary War, General Richard Richardson was imprisoned by the British, but was allowed to return home to die. He was buried there in the cemetery. Not long after Richardson's death, Lt. Col. Banastre Tarleton, demanded that General Richardson's body be dug up. He claimed that it was so he could "look on the face of such a noble man," but it was because he wanted to force the General's widow to reveal the whereabouts of General Francis Marion, the Swamp Fox. Walter Edgar, a noted South Carolina historian, has indicated that in all likelihood the body was mutilated in the presence of the widow. True to her late husband's convictions, she never revealed any information about Marion.

Entombed in the cemetery is Richard Richardson, Brigadier in the American Revolution; James Burchell Richardson, South Carolina Governor 1802-04; and John Peter Richardson, South Carolina Governor 1840-42 and founder of the Citadel; and the widow who refused to reveal information to the enemy.

The most Governors to ever be elected in South Carolina from one family were from the Manning/Richardson family of Clarendon County.

The Big Home burial grounds, long the final resting place for generations of the Richardson family, can be recognized from some distance away by the tall white stones.

water that for centuries has been used for water power. Tradition holds that a long time ago an afternoon storm came up and blew over a tree pinning a worker. He was drowned and his body was brought out of the swamp and laid out on the floor at the mill house to await the coroner. As a result locals will not under any circumstances cross the dam to the mill pond after dark. Just a legend? Well, anyway you have been warned!

Today the old mill pond is a thing of beauty with moss filled cypress trees. The water is covered with duck weed, a floating plant, and adds to the mystery of the area.

Just before the SC Waterfowl Association headquarters, the trail ducks back into the woods. Kudzu is thick here and often covers the trail. Back on Santee Cooper lands the forest closes in with a dense canopy from the huge trees.

At Packs Landing a trailhead offers parking, supplies and information. The trail reenters via a boardwalk and the forest closes in quickly. About a quarter mile past Packs Landing and off to the right there is a primitive camp site on high ground. It's a couple hundred yards over to the site and the trail over can be wet with standing water after rains. Along this most primitive section, look for alligators and snakes.

You climb a slow incline in grade on the trail and a pond appears on the right with turtles and alligators. As you pass a stream measuring station on your right, there are usually some really big cottonmouth snakes sunning.

The trail passes through some really wet ground and is elevated on split logs. In late summer the jewelweed covers the area and is often waist high. The juice from the stems of the plant has fungicidal properties and is a well known treatment for poison ivy and stinging nettle.

As the trail follows closely along the waterline, look out over Sparkleberry Swamp on the left. Sparkleberry Landing is a trailhead for day use and the launching of expeditions into the swamp.

Use your map for the next mile or

Today Halfway Swamp is a place of beauty to some and to others it's a place of mystery and haunting. The dam at the mill pond forms a lake and the water surface fills with duck weed forming a green mat around the cypress trees.

Rimini

The little village of Rimini sprung up on the Old River Road which served as the stage road from Camden to Georgetown. The origins of the name and the spelling are somewhat lost. It would appear that a work crew of Italian descent worked on the railroad or logging industry or possibly both and named the village after a town on the seacoast of Italy.

Logging of the vast forest of pine and cypress was a major industry and supported the community for more than a century. In the late 1800's Rimini was a boom town. Logging crews worked to fell the vast cypress forest in the swamp. These forests lined the old Santee River channel. The Cypress Lumber Company floated the logs down the river to their big lumber mill at Ferguson. Several lumber mills operated on the high land around Rimini and shipped their pine boards by rail.

Cotton and corn were the main agricultural crops. Halfway Swamp was dammed and floodgates installed to operate a gristmill and later a cotton gin. The water power was even used to power a saw mill. Legend has it that while cutting trees in the mill pond, a storm blew a tree on a worker. He was pinned in the shallow water but drowned before help arrived to remove the tree.

His body was brought out and laid on the floor of the cotton gin to await the coroner. This gave rise to the belief that the place is haunted. Local people in the community will not to this day cross the dam after night fall. The Palmetto Trail crosses the dam on the Old River Road.

The industry that Rimini is most famous for isn't talked about much. It is said that during Prohibition "Rimini cocktails" were served in New York and Washington, DC. The corn whisky was bootleg and illegal but of excellent quality. The wild and remote areas along the swamps were ideal for a thriving industry out of the sight of the "Revenuers." Today as you travel the Palmetto Trail you'll see old rusty barrels that have been chopped with axes when the moonshine stills were destroyed by the federal agents.

Today, Rimini is little more than a wide spot in the road. It's located on the Sumter/Clarendon County line where the railroad crosses Camp Mac Boykin Road and intersects with the Old River Road and Governor Richardson Road. There is one store but they have the promise of a super highway connecting them with Lone Star on the other side of the lake.

so as the trail follows rural country roads before darting into the Manchester State Forest. Once into the forest the terrain changes considerably on the trail. Ravines, side slopes and ridge tops are found at almost every turn. The forest floor is rich with a variety of plants. You may even see the Roseling, a delicate pink flower in the

spiderwort family that is found along the inner coastal plain. Thickets of sparkleberry bushes close in on the trail and the overstory is oak, hickory and pine.

Sparkleberry is a unique shrub or in some cases a small tree. It's not all that common but can be found almost throughout the state. A member of the

Though rare in the Coastal Plain a covering of snow can change the orinary into the extraordinary. Hiking the Palmetto Trail right after a snow can be a real treat.

blueberry family, the leaves are leathery and a dark shiny green often turning a rich purple reddish in the autumn. The snow white flowers appear in early May and are arranged in profuse drooping clusters. During colonial times weddings often would be timed to coincide with the blooming of the sparkleberry so the beautiful flowers could be used by the bride.

The trail drops down a slope to a wet seepage and crosses on a narrow boardwalk. The trees are wetland species and the bog is covered with sphagnum moss and evergreen shrubs.

At Mill Creek County Park the trail emerges on the day use side which serves as the trailhead.

People and Places

You're now in the heart of Santee Cooper Country; a five county region promoted for fishing, boating, hiking, hunting and golf. Two lakes, two rivers, two canals and a vast swamp – Santee Cooper is awesome. Lake Marion and Lake Moultrie are famous for the

landlocked striped bass. Along with stripers, largemouth bass, crappie, bream, and catfish are in abundance to challenge the fisherman.

The pace is slow and the people are friendly. If you find that you want to stay awhile you will find full service motels, lake cabins and over 1,000 camp sites. Dining is an experience. You can sample good old Southern home cooking, traditional barbecue or a local favorite, fried catfish. The writers with Backpacker Magazine hiked the Lake Marion Passage of the Palmetto Trail and entitled their article "Country Fried Hike,"

If you want a comfortable room in Santee you will find **Clark's Inn**, 114 Bradford Blvd., Santee, SC 29142, (803) 854-2141 or (800) 531-9658. It has been renovated and decorated in traditional bed & breakfast style, and offers all the comforts of home. **Quality Inn & Suites**, 8929 Bass Dr., Santee, SC 29142, (803) 854-2121 or (800) 880-2121. Their rooms have been decorated in true Southern style to include plantation style windows and doors. The restaurant is the **Carolina Grill**, a full service restaurant serving breakfast and dinner daily. A slew of motels and eateries line Old Number Six Hwy in Santee and offer a break from the trail.

Jacks Creek Marina is a gem on the shore of Lake Marion and a great place to stop-over. Located on the south side of Jacks Creek, tent camp sites overlook the lake and you can wake to the sounds of waterfowl. They can be contacted at Jacks Creek Marina, 2226 Jacks Creek Rd., Summerton, South Carolina 29148, 803-478-2793. **Carolina King Retreat and Marina** (formerly Billups Landing) offers cabin rentals (no tent camping) if you want a place to hold-up while day hiking or biking. They are on the north side of Jacks Creek and can be contacted at Carolina King Retreat & Marina, 2498 Belser Road, Summerton, SC 29148, 800-451-5313 or 803-478-2800.

Elloree is located just west of Santee on Old Number Six Hwy and over the last 200 years the community has grown from a two-rut dirt road to the river to a community which is becoming a tourist destination for golf, fishing, hunting, horse racing, boating (canoeing and kayaking), wildlife photography, camping, tennis and shopping.

The town has completed a revitalization project by installing new streets, sidewalks and median with brick trim, shade trees, benches and flowers and new street lamps. The 1900 era buildings are now being renovated to become homes to antique and specialty shops, art galleries and cafes. This is a great place to spend some time just relaxing, eating and shopping.

Santee National Wildlife Refuge
A birders paradise

This beautiful nature preserve has 15,000 acres of uplands, waterfowl impoundments and open waters of Lake Marion. Managed for migratory waterfowl, a myriad of wildlife inhabit the varied landscape of the Santee National Wildlife Refuge.

The winter months bring geese and a variety of ducks along with bald eagles and occasionally a peregrine falcon. Year-round residents are the hawks, numerous songbirds and wild turkeys. The ponds and marshes are home to some really big alligators.

There are a number of natural and cultural resources located on the refuge. Dingle Pond is a true Carolina Bay. Scattered through the southeastern coastal plain, they are a puzzling, unsolved geological phenomenon whose origins are lost in folklore. Ft. Watson is an Indian ceremonial and burial mound. During the American Revolutionary War the British constructed an outpost and fort on the top. The Americans constructed a tower during darkness and at daybreak routed the British in April of 1781.

Santee National Wildlife Refuge
2125 Ft. Watson Road
Summerton, SC 29148
(803) 478-2217

Santee State Park
A nature-based destination

Santee State Park is located in the heart of Santee Cooper Country with 2,496 acres of nature-based excitement. Located on the south shore of Lake Marion, the park offers pier-based cabins, camp sites, recreational trails, nature programs and a great nature display.

Lake Marion's "flooded forest" across from the park is just one of the attractions that draws fishermen, bird watchers, swamp lovers and boaters under power or sail. Fish Eagle boat provides tours on a regular schedule. Call (803) 854-4005.

Santee State Park
251 State Park Road

Santee, SC 29142
(803) 854-2408

Sparkleberry Swamp
Fresh water swamp of unusual beauty

Sparkleberry Swamp consists of a 16,000 acre tract and is located in the headwaters of Lake Marion where the Wateree and Congaree Rivers converge. It's a true natural treasure - a gem brimming with wildlife, publicly accessible, offering a great outdoor experience for paddlers and fishermen. The slow, twisty creeks and tall cypress trees make everything look alike and it's easy to lose your way. There is no specific trail to follow and a visitor can spend endless hours meandering through the swamp.

Sparkleberry Swamp is a true natural treasure, a gem brimming with wildlife, offering a great outdoor experience for paddlers and fishermen.

Before 1942 when the Lake Marion Dam was completed, Sparkleberry Swamp was similar to the Congaree Swamp in that it had more dry land than wet. Now the situation is reversed, and the swamp is permanently inundated with water. This significantly altered the original habitat of the swamp but has done nothing to detract from its natural beauty.

The put-in point is Sparkleberry Landing, which is off of Camp Mac Boykin Road in Sumter County. Turn right on a dirt road if you are heading south on Camp Mac Boykin Road. The turn is about 4.5 miles south of the junction of Camp Mac Boykin Road and SC Hwy 261. There is a boat landing and good parking area which serves as a trailhead for the Palmetto Trail. Check the water level before going paddling in the swamp. A water level below 74 feet will expose numerous submerged logs and shallows.

Historic Liberty Hill AME Church
An Uncommon Courage

The Liberty Hill AME Church fostered the origins of Briggs-DeLaine law suit which led to desegregation in area schools across the south. The meetings held here in the 1940's and 50's resulted in the case *Harry Briggs, Jr., vs R.W. Elliott.* Nineteen members of the congregation were plaintiffs in the case heard in U.S. District Court in 1952 at Charleston. This case was later rolled into others and heard before the US Supreme Court, resulting in the 1954 landmark decision desegregating public schools. Read more about the *Briggs vs. Elliott* case in *Uncommon Courage* by PCF Press.

The church is located one mile north of St. Paul, SC on secondary road 373 just off the trail in Clarendon County.

Halfway Swamp

The Battle of Halfway Swamp occurred on February 1781. The Americans were pursuing a policy of making dangerous the line between Charleston and Camden. General Marion met the 64th British Regiment at Halfway Swamp. Major Robert McLeroth, considered to be the most humane of all

British commanders, accepted Marion's challenge to determine the battle with twenty selected men from each side. When the twenty men were ready to do battle, a British officer road forward, and the British army shouldered their muskets and retreated. McLeroth had used the plan as a ruse to consume daylight and slip away under cover of darkness.

The first St. Mark's Church was located at Halfway Swamp. Today the site is a beautiful mill pond with moss filled cypress trees and green duck weed covering the pond.

Outfitters and Nature Guides

Fish Eagle is a nature-based boat tour operating out of Santee State Park with daily trips into the "sunken forest" in Lake Marion. You can get up close and personal with the natural flora and fauna of the lake. Visit the tackle shop for supplies or rent a bike, canoe, kayak or a John Boat.
Fish Eagle Tours
PO Box 1086
Santee, SC 29142
(803) 854-4005

The Local Eateries

Clark's Restaurant (8920 Old Hwy #6, 803-854-2101) offering Southern cuisine and "spirits" in a pub-like atmosphere is located in the heart of Santee. For almost 60 years, travelers and locals have enjoyed excellent food and "spirits" as well as the Southern charm and ambience of Clark's. Open daily for breakfast, lunch and dinner, they offer a variety of exceptional traditional cuisine - wonderful seafood, stir-fry, as well as an abundance of comfort foods. Fireside dining, a charming courtyard, meeting and banquet rooms are just a few of their extras.

Captain Kirk's Steak & Seafood Grill (917 Resort Street, 803- 854-2025) offers some of the very best seafood dishes around. In fact that is their specialty. You can also get steaks, chicken or chops and a ½ lb. ground chuck hamburger. Oh yeah, they have grits as well. You can find them just east of Santee off Old Number Six Hwy at the Lake Marion Resort & Marina, 917 Resort Street, Santee, SC (803) 854-2025. Open Tuesday – Saturday at 4:30 pm. You may want to call ahead for seating.

The Tastee Food Shop Restaurant (656 Bass Dr., 803-854-2272) serves steaks, seafood, fried chicken, roast beef, turkey, ham, and 10-12 vegetables every day along with soups and salads. Breakfast is served anytime. Portions are generous and reasonably priced. No smoking. You will find them located right on the trail in Santee and adjacent to Mansion Park Motor Lodge.

Food Lion Grocery (697 Bass Drive, 803-854-2274) offers a Supermarket Deli section featuring daily specials for take out.

In Summerton are the **Summerton Diner** (325 Church Street 803-485-6835) and the **Sunshine Restaurant** (2 N. Cantey Street 803-485-8709) both worth stopping by.

Produce

You will often find produce vendors set up along the highways and street corners. They feature fresh grown fruits and vegetables. Just about a mile north of Summerton on US 15 is a produce stand. Local farms in the Clarendon County area are growing more and more tomatoes, squash, beans, sweet corn, and greens plus blackberries, blueberries, strawberries, peaches and the like. East of Santee are several really good produce stands on Old Number Six Hwy.

Convenience Stores

Rivers Country Store (8851 Old Number Six Hwy., 803-854-2965) has been the fishermen and hunters' supply center for generations. Tackle, bait (live and otherwise), hunting gear and special items are displayed for easy shopping. Clothing items are of good quality with many name brands available.

Santee General Store (8932 Old Number Six Hwy., 803-854-2405) is a landmark in Santee. For years, travelers have stopped for delicious hand dipped ice cream cones in flavors that remind you of your childhood. Fireworks and souvenirs are available at reasonable prices. They have the best selection of jellies, preserves, hot sauces, dressings and ciders and offer a wide variety of hunting and fishing supplies.

Smith's Chevron is the place to get anything you may be looking for to take with you. Anything from cider, pecans, fireworks, souvenirs, jelly, southern fried peanuts and salad dressings is available. Located on Old Number Six Hwy to the east of I-95 you can't miss it. Call (800) 439-1485.

Local Artisans

During April of each year in conjunction with the Striped Bass Festival some 70 high quality artisans and crafters will surround the courthouse square in Manning, SC offering some of the South's best wares. Call (803) 435-4405 for more information. The noted newscaster, the late Walter Winchell, once called Manning "the prettiest town from Maine to Miami." Check it out as you will find the people friendly.

Or take a short break from hiking or biking and check out the Town of Elloree which has become home to antique and specialty shops, art galleries and cafes.

The pace is slow and you can relax and shop without all the rush of a mall. It's a unique shopping experience. Call (803) 897-2821, Elloree's Town Hall for more information.

Summerton is another town just

begging for a stop to bourse around. Hidden in the antique and junk shops may be just the find you are looking for your home. You will find the shopping worth your time and some really good eats.

Much of the Palmetto Trail is maintained by volunteers. Annually countless hours are contributed by enthusiastic trail advocates.

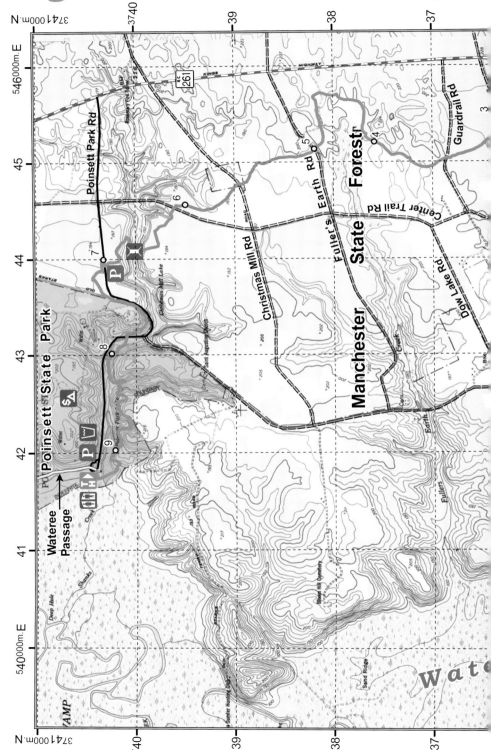

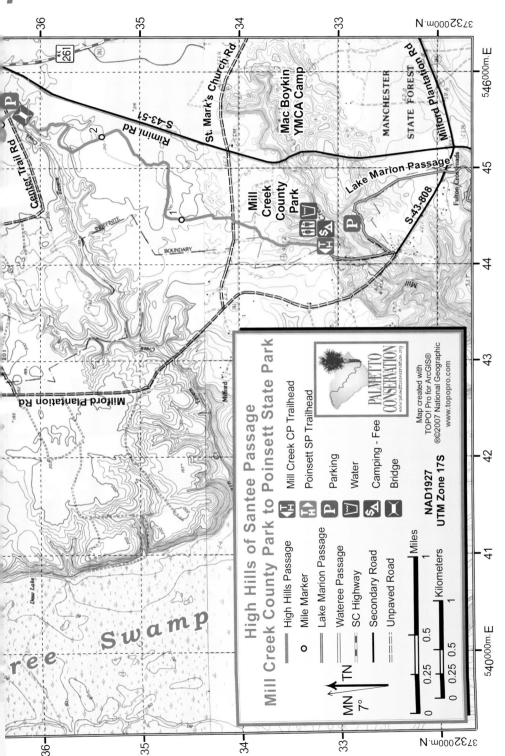

SC 261

Center Trail Rd

Rimini Rd
S-43-51

St. Mark's Church Rd

Mac Boykin
YMCA Camp

MANCHESTER

STATE FOREST

Milford Plantation Rd

Lake Marion Passage

Mill
Creek
County
Park

S-43-808

Fulton Crossroads

P

BOUNDARY

INDEFINITE

Milford Plantation Rd

Dew Lake

Swamp

ree

High Hills of Santee Passage
Mill Creek County Park to Poinsett State Park

	High Hills Passage		Mill Creek CP Trailhead
o	Mile Marker		Poinsett SP Trailhead
	Lake Marion Passage		Parking
	Wateree Passage		Water
	SC Highway		Camping - Fee
	Secondary Road		Bridge
	Unpaved Road		

NAD1927
UTM Zone 17S

Miles

Kilometers

MN
7°

TN

Map created with
TOPO! Pro for ArcGIS®
®©2007 National Geographic
www.topopro.com

PALMETTO
CONSERVATION
www.palmettoconservation.org

3732000m.N

36
35
34
33

546000m.E
45
44
43
42
41
540000m.E

High Hills of the Santee Passage

The High Hills of the Santee Passage, through a unique partnership with the Manchester State Forest, Poinsett State Park and Mill Creek County Park, covers one of the most historic sections of the trail. A multi-use trail for hikers, mountain bikers, and equestrians, the trail is steeped in history. One can feel the presence of Catawba Indians, early settlers and explorers, plantation owners, traders and travelers of the past. Numerous Revolutionary War tales, unmarked historic sites, plantations and ruins from the past await the trail user.

The 9 mile segment adjacent to the Wateree River swamp was named after the high, sandy ridges on the trail which was at one time part of the Catawba trail. This passage is ideal for horseback riding, hiking, bird watching, camping and mountain biking.

Trail enthusiasts will marvel at the hilly topography, home to a diversity of plants and animals. The trail passes one the rare places where mountain laurel flowers grow beneath a veil of Spanish moss. Red cedar, oaks, dogwood, pine and wildlife are abundant in the densely wooded hilly terrain.

High Hills of the Santee lie wholly within a geographic region known as the Sandhills of South Carolina and are a narrow band of rolling hills in portions of Aiken, Lexington, Richland, Sumter, and Kershaw Counties. The Sandhills overlap what is known as the Fall Line, which runs northeast - southwest through the Midlands and separates the Piedmont and Coastal Plain. Millions of years ago, the sea covered a large portion of eastern and southern South Carolina and its shoreline corresponded to the present day sand hills. Examples of these ancient dunes can be

The High Hills of the Santee Passage, named after the high sandy ridges of the Manchester State Forest, was at one time part of the Catawba trail. Here the hilly topography and the diversity of plants and animals are a delight for the trail user.

seen all along the High Hills Passage, south of Wedgefield and north of Pinewood in the Manchester State Forest. And in several areas, the trail cuts through the tops of old beach ridges.

The picturesque sand hill area of western Sumter County has been long known as the "High Hills of the Santee." Englishman, John Lawson who explored the area in 1701 gave the earliest account of the High Hills. He thought that they were mountains and described them as amazing. The "Alp with a top like a Sugar-loaf," he wrote, as he viewed the hills across a beautiful swamp twenty miles wide. It is believed that he was atop Cook's Mount, opposite Stateburg. In years to come, once the area that was to eventually be known as Sumter County became more settled, the gentry of the Lowcountry began to spend their summers in the High Hills of the Santee. Previously they had taken their families to the northern colonies to escape the hot and humid weather of the coast. The sandhills area where Poinsett Park, Mill Creek Park, Manchester Forest and St. Marks Church are located, constitute the southern end of the High Hills of the Santee and was first inhabited by planters and their families as their summer home. Their winter homes were far back, toward the rivers, where the swamps were infested with malaria, during the warm months.

Difficulty: Moderately easy however the soft sands may present a problem for hikers and mountain bikers.

Length: 9 miles

Fees: No fee required for hikers but mountain bikers and equestrian users are required to have a permit from the state forest.

Conditions: June through September is the hot summer season and high temperatures and high humidity can be a problem. Biting insects along this passage are a real problem. Snakes and alligators call the ecosystem home, including the venomous snake varieties. Potable water is available at the Mill Creek County Park and Poinsett State Park.

USGS Quadrangles: Poinsett and Lone Star

Directions: *For Poinsett State Park;* From the junction of SC Hwy. 378 and SC Hwy. 261 S., 28 miles from Columbia, 16 miles from Sumter, travel ten miles south on SC 261 to Poinsett Park Road (S-43-63), turn right (west), travel 1.3 miles to River Road; turn right for a tenth of a mile; equestrian campground is on the left.

For hiking and biking day-use parking, park at Poinsett State park, entrance on S-43-63. For equestrian day-use, park on River Road north of S-43-63.

Manchester State Forest offers trailhead parking (day use) for the Palmetto Trail and mountain bike trails on the left on Poinsett Park Road just before entering Poinsett State Park.

For Mill Creek Park; From the junction of SC Hwy. 378 and SC Hwy.

261 S., 28 miles from Columbia, 16 miles from Sumter, travel 12.5 miles south on SC 261 to S-43-51 (Camp Mac Boykin Road), take right-hand fork (sign says: to Rimini); travel three miles to S-43-808 (Millford Plantation Road), turn right (west); travel .8 miles to Mill Creek Park entrance. Turn right (north) into Park; bear right .3 miles to day-use parking area.

Hours: Year-round. Night hiking permitted

Camping: Tent camping and cabins are available at Poinsett State Park. Tent sites rent for $9 - $10 per night, $13 with electricity. Cabins rent for $40 - $98 per night. Contact the park at (803) 494-8177. Camping is available at Mill Creek County Park. Contact the park management at 7975 Millford Plantation Road, Pinewood, SC 29125, (803) 436-2248.

Information: Contact Manchester State Forest, 7640 Headquarters Road Wedgefield, SC 29168,(803) 494-8196

Poinsett State Park, 6660 Poinsett Park Road, Wedgefield, SC 29168 (803) 494-8177

Mill Creek County Park, 7975 Millford Plantation Road, Pinewood, SC 29125 (803) 436-2248

Palmetto Conservation, 1314 Lincoln Street, Suite 305, Columbia, SC 29201-3154, (803)-771-0870

On the Trail

The user has several options to access the 14 mile High Hill of the Santee Passage. At Mill Creek the trail enters from the south at the day-use side and then loops around the pond and exits on the camping side to the north.

Here at Mill Creek the trail becomes multi-use with hikers, bikers and equestrians on this passage. The trail gets heavy use from horses and the sandy soils in the trail tread become quite soft. Poinsett offers separate trails for equestrians and the Palmetto Trail is limited to hikers and bikers. Here the trail tread is firm and compact. The Palmetto Trail on the Manchester State Forest in places can be difficult for hikers and bikers because of the horse hooves breaking the trail tread.

From Mill Creek the trail follows the sandy ridges through pines forests of longleaf pine and turkey oak. The plant community is interesting. Turkey oak is the primary oak that has adapted to the dry sands. In the spring lupine is common with the blue spike flowers. Hog plums and hawthorn both have edible though very tart berries which are great for making jellies and jams. Milkweed, phlox, prickly pear cactus and nettles dot the forest floor. The yellow jessamine, the state flower of South Carolina, climbs trees and bushes and blooms in profusion in the late winter and spring.

The trail dips down and crosses Tavern Creek on a bridge and then up to a staging area for equestrian users. This trailhead can be accessed from SC 261 on Center Trail Road.

The trail continues to wind through the pine forest and crosses Fullers Earth Creek. Fuller's earth is natural clay like substance that is used in a number of applications. It is non-plastic in properties and is highly absorbent of basic colors and oils. A short distance south of here it once was mined as "kitty litter" but has numerous other uses.

The vegetation changes abruptly as the trail crosses the creeks because of water seepage feeding the small creeks. Fetterbush, staggerbush, doghobble and cane are evergreen shrubs that form dense thickets along the creeks. An overstory of black gum, yellow poplar, red bay and maple create a refreshing respite from the dry sandy ridges in the summer.

The High Hills of the Santee Passage offers a large diversity of plants that thrive on the dry sandy soils like the lupine with flowers arranged in mounds of blue spikes.

The trail crosses Shanks Creek and out to the trailhead on Poinsett Park Road (paved). The trailhead was designed for equestrian users but is never used by that group. However it also serves as a trailhead for some really great mountain bike trails. The Campbell Pond, Hardcore and the Killer Three mountain bike trails are a real challenge for the bikers. Plus they cover some really great terrain through interesting woods with well packed trail treads. Hikers can access the Palmetto Trail from the trailhead.

As you cross the River Road (dirt) you enter Poinsett State Park. Back to your right is an equestrian camp site that gets very little use. The equestrian, biking and hiking trails on the state park are single use trails.

The Palmetto Trail turns back to your left (hiking and biking only) and begins a descent down into the park. The terrain becomes mountainous and the vegetation is a mix of coastal plain and mountain species. Mountain laurel grows under trees with Spanish moss. Thickets of sparkleberry line the trail.

Geocaching

Geocaching is an outdoor treasure hunting game in which the participants use a global positioning system or GPS receiver to hide and seek containers called geocaches or caches. A typical cache is a small waterproof container containing a logbook and "treasure," usually toys or trinkets of little monetary value.

Geocaching is similar to a much older activity called letterboxing. The major difference is its use of the global positioning system. The activity has been made possible by recent satellite technology.

As an entertaining adventure game, participating in a cache hunt is a good way to take advantage of the wonderful features and capability of a GPS unit. The basic idea is to have individuals and organizations set up caches along the trail and share the locations of these caches on the internet. GPS users can then use the location coordinates to find the caches. Once found, a cache may provide the visitor with a wide variety of rewards. All the visitor is asked to do is if they take something, they should leave something for the cache.

The GPS unit is an electronic device that can determine your approximate location (within 6-20 feet) on the planet. Coordinates are normally given in longitude and latitude. You can use the unit to navigate from your current location to another location. Some units have their own maps, built-in electronic compasses, voice navigation, all depending on the complexity of the device.

You don't need to know all the technical mumbo jumbo about GPS units to go geocaching. All you need to do is be able to enter what is called a "waypoint" where the geocache is hidden.

GPS Units range from $100 to $1000 depending on the kind of capabilities the user would like. The basic units run for around $100 and can get you to within 20 feet of any geocache. The next step up is a unit with a built-in electronic compass, topographic maps, and much more memory capacity.

You can usually find GPS units at any boat supply, outdoor supply or electronic store. A good, basic GPS unit is the Garman e Trex GPS or the Magellan GPS 315.

Geocaching is a relatively new

The trails within the park are well designed and offer a challenging hiking experience. Mostly built by the Civilian Conservation Corps in the 1930's, the shelters date from their work in establishing Poinsett. The vistas are magnificent and much more than you would expect in the coastal plain.

The park headquarters is on the north side of the Levi Mill Pond and the trail crosses the dam.

People and Places

The Natural Thing to Do!

Sumter County abounds in scenic beauty, an irresistible enticement for nature lovers. Family fun and relaxation, adventures in challenging the elements, and everything in between awaits the visitor. The scenic beauty and sun-soaked climate offer the best in outdoor fun year round, and there's always something exciting to do! Located in the upper coastal plain and sandhills region of the state, Sumter

phenomenon. There are some simple rules that participants should observe. If you take something from the cache you should leave something. Make an entry with the date and time you visited in the logbook and replace the cache.

The contents of a cache can vary considerably but the first item should always be the logbook. Some caches can be just a logbook and nothing else. The logbook contains information from the founder of the cache and notes from the cache's visitors. A logbook might contain information about nearby attractions, coordinates to other unpublished caches, and even jokes written by visitors.

The location of a cache can be very entertaining and challenging. As is often said, location, location, location! The location of a cache demonstrates the founder's skill and possibly even daring. A cache located on the side of a rocky cliff accessible only by rock climbing equipment may be hard to find. An underwater cache may only be accessed by scuba. Other caches may require long difficult hiking,

orienteering, and special equipment to get to.

All along the Palmetto Trail are geocaches. These hidden treasures are at numerous locations unnoticed by the casual trail user. More caches are being hidden every week and there are an increasing number of users participating in the treasure hunts. You can search the internet for coordinates to find caches. To start your fun and get basic information you can log on to www.geocaching.com.

Geocaching is an outdoor treasure hunting game in which the particpants use a global positioning system or GPS receiver to hide and seek containers called geocaches or caches.

County's forest, rushing rivers and scenic lakes are a real treat to delight the senses.

Boating, birding, hiking, biking, fishing, hunting and horseback riding come naturally to most residents and visitors. The world-famous Swan Lake Iris Gardens feature all eight known swan species and the most intensive plantings of Japanese iris in the United States. Manchester State Forest is home to annual equestrian events, mountain biking and ATV trails, the High Hills and Wateree Passages of the Palmetto Trail and some of the best hunting in the state.

Poinsett State Park offers a near mountain experience with some excellent trails.

Spend some time here and take an outdoor journey through Sumter County… it's the natural thing to do.

Manchester State Forest
A true forest

The Manchester State Forest is located in Sumter and Clarendon Counties, on the fall line between the piedmont and coastal plan. The forest consists of more than 25,000 acres of ridges, ancient sand dunes, hardwood bottoms, bays, and swampland with mixed pine and hardwood species native to South Carolina. It is a highly diverse, magnificent forest, rich in timber, plants, and wildlife.

Manchester State Forest practices principles of high quality multiple-use and sustained-yield forest management. The forest is managed to yield a variety of forest products, from pulpwood and sawtimber to poles and pine straw and wildlife. Stands of non-native slash pine, planted in the 1960s, are being gradually harvested and replaced with longleaf pine.

Recreational use of the forest continues to increase as a popular destination. Hunting, fishing, horseback riding, motorcycle/ATV riding and mountain biking are among the favorite activities. Separate trails have been designed for horses, mountain bikes, and motorcycles and ATVs.

Recreational use permits have been implemented and are mandatory for all trails for riding including horseback riding, biking, and motorcycle and ATV's. Recreational hiking is exempt from the permit system.

Manchester State Forest
7640 Headquarters Road
Wedgefield, SC 29168
(803) 494-8196

In Poinsett State Park the terrain becomes mountainous and the vegetation is a mix of coastal plain and mountain species. Mountain laurel grows under trees with Spanish moss. Thickets of sparkleberry line the trail.

Poinsett State Park
Diversity beyond description

Poinsett State Park is located in an outlying area of the Sandhills, yet is still within the coastal plain. The park's terrain allows for an amazing diversity of plant and animal life. Plant communities represented within the park include sandhills, swamps, mountain bluffs and pine-hardwood. Mountain laurel and galax grow on steep facing hillsides, while Spanish-moss-draped cypress and tupelo trees rise from the swamp. This 1,000-acre park, with its abundant resources, and a nature center with a full-time naturalist, is an excellent laboratory for outdoor education.

The campground has 50 sites which can accommodate RV's. There are four cabins available for rental. There is an equestrian campground. Five picnic shelters are available and can be reserved for a fee. The nature center includes displays on native Sumter County animals, plants and history. There are several hiking trails, an equestrian trail and a bike trail. You can enjoy fishing in the park's 10-acre Levi Mill Pond for bass, bream and catfish. Fishing boats can be rented but no private boats are permitted.

The yellow jessamine, the state flower in South Carolina, climbs trees and bushes and blooms in profusion in the late winter and spring.

The Poinsett State Park headquarters is on the north side of the Levi Mill Pond and the trail crosses the dam. Poinsett offers bathrooms and potable water.

Poinsett State Park
6660 Poinsett Park Road
Wedgefield, SC 29168
(803) 494-8177

St. Marks Episcopal Church

The first church to be organized in Sumter District was the Parish Church for St. Marks Parish. The origins of St. Marks church can be traced back to 1757 with the formation of the Parish. The original building was constructed in 1765 and only served the congregation for a few years before being burned by Tarleton's troops. Various calamities continued to befall the church. The present building was completed in 1856 and is the fourth church building to serve St. Marks Parish. This beautiful sanctuary, located near SC Hwy 261 in the Manchester State Forest on the Camp Mac Boykin Road, has been a house of worship for six South Carolina governors. Regular services are no longer held, but the simple, elegant building stands as a reminder of an important time in South Carolina history.

The first church organized in the Sumter District was the Parish Church for St. Marks Parish. The present building dates from 1856 and has been a house of worship for six South Carolina Governors.

The Local Eateries

A little off the trail in Pinewood is Linda's Grill right on SC Hwy 261. Featuring a buffet or off the menu items, it's real home cooking. Decorated with "Elvis" memorabilia, you can relax and enjoy your meal or strike up a conversation with John. Convenient if you are on the Lake Marion or the High Hills Passages. They are open early for breakfast and oh, yeah, don't miss the fried chicken.

Linda's Grill
Intersection of Clark St and SC 261
Pinewood, SC
(803) 452-6757

Linda's Grill right on SC Hwy. 261 in Pinewood features real home cooking and opens early. It's convenient if you are on the Lake Marion or the High Hills Passages.

Wateree Passage

The Wateree Passage is without question one of the most diverse passages of the Palmetto Trail. The 7 mile passage leaves from Poinsett State Park, winds its way through near mountainous terrain and at one point reaches one of the highest elevations in Sumter County, over 270 feet above sea level.

The Manchester State Forest and the Wateree River floodplain contain most of the trail. The abandoned railroad bed carries the user deep within the swamp among towering hardwood and cypress trees, creeks, numerous snakes and a great variety of animal and bird life.

The rich alluvial soils grow large trees and the shade from the canopy keeps the forest floor relatively free of underbrush. More than 300 plant species have been identified, many not expected in the area. The numerous creeks offer excellent fishing.

Bird species will vary with the seasons but ever present is the sound of the Barred owl. You can get them to answer you with a loud hoot. The creeks often offer a fleeting glimpse of the Prothonotary warbler.

Difficulty: Moderately difficult

Length: 7 miles

Fees: No fee required for hikers but mountain bike users are required to have a permit from the state forest.

Conditions: The different seasons make a really big change in conditions. High temperatures and high humidity can be a problem during the summer months. The winter winds can be quite biting in the swamp. Insects along this passage are often present but not a real problem. During some seasons the imported lady bugs are present in large numbers. Snakes and alligators call the ecosystem home, including the venomous snake varieties. They especially like to sun on the trestles and as the ballast from the old railroad warms snakes seek out the warmth. Potable water is available at the Poinsett State Park.

USGS Quadrangles: Poinsett

Directions: *For Poinsett Park;* From US Hwy. 378 near Sumter, take SC 261 south through Wedgefield for 10 miles. Turn right onto Poinsett State Park Rd. and go 2.7 miles to the lake. The kiosk at the park office is where the Wateree Passage connects to the High Hills Passage.

For Foxville Rd. Parking Area: From US 378 near Sumter, take SC 261 south through Wedgefield for 5.8 miles. Turn right onto Middleton Rd. opposite Orangehill Church. Paved road becomes unpaved after 1.4 miles; continue 1.2 miles. Turn left and another immediate left onto Foxville Rd. (unmarked). Take left fork at .7 miles; .7 miles further is a small parking area with a kiosk on the left, yellow gate to the right. Note: Foxville Rd. is deeply rutted in places and may not be suitable for vehicles with low ground clearance.

For Campbell Creek Rd. Parking Area: From US 378 near Sumter, take SC 261 south through Wedgefield for 8.1 miles.

An abandoned railroad bed carries the user deep within the Wateree Swamp among towering trees, creeks, numerous snakes and a great variety of animal and bird life.

Manchester

Manchester was once a flourishing town on the high ground along the Wateree Swamp. The town was settled sometime before 1799 and became a center of commerce because of its location. The town flourished and served as a shipping center for cotton by boat to Charleston. In 1840 it was listed as one of the largest towns in South Carolina. The landing was nearby and was the head of navigation. Buyers met traders in Manchester. The wares were loaded onto boats and then carried down the Wateree to the Santee River, through the Santee Canal to the Cooper River, and on to Charleston.

It also served as a stage-coach stop on the road to Charleston and from 1852 – 1872 was a busy station on the Wilmington and Manchester Railroad. All that remains of the town today is an iron historical marker on SC Hwy 261 about three miles south of Wedgefield.

The town was laid out in an orderly fashion, the land was cleared and stately homes built. As many as ten stores were in business at one time. The streets were given names like King Street, Queen Street, and Main Road. The people moving to Manchester in the early years were planters. Eventually, the farms became great estates along the river. Manchester was a place for amusement and entertainment and where families moved to avoid the fevers of the swamp.

Cotton was grown on the high lands and rice was grown in the swamp. As the markets in Charleston and elsewhere demanded more and more, the planters grew very rich. Large numbers of cattle and hogs were raised annually in the swamp for the markets in Charleston and along the Atlantic coast.

The building of the town attracted tradesman and artisans. There were

All that remains of the town of Manchester is an iron historical marker along Highway SC 261 that marks the site of the once flourishing center of commerce.

shopkeepers, seamstresses, tailors, cobblers, a doctor, postmaster and a cotton factory. A tavern sprang up for the travelers and soon became notorious. Early on, the river trade attracted large numbers of men to load and handle the boats.

Manchester was on the Kings Highway leading from the mountains to Charleston and a never ending stream of wagons passed through the town. Yankee peddlers traveled the country side peddling their wares.

The town became noted for its taverns, the horse-racing, games of ball-alley and cock-fighting. The wealthy had money and time and indulged in pleasures. Soon Manchester became know as a by-word for all that was wicked and sinful.

The town often was referred to as the Sodom and Gomorrah of the Sumter District.

Today the town has all but vanished except for the name and the tales of promise, prosperity, and decay.

Turn right onto the dirt Range Rd./ Campbell Creek Rd. and go 2.6 miles to the intersection with Tiveton Church Rd. (unmarked). This wide intersection is the parking area. From here it's a half mile hike along the old railroad bed to the Palmetto Trail. If traveling north on SC 261, Campbell Creek Rd./Range Road is 1.7 miles from the Poinsett Park Road. Turn left and go 2.6 miles to the wide intersection with Tiveton Church Rd.

Hours: Year-round. Night hiking permitted

Camping: Camping and cabins are available at Poinsett State Park. Tent sites rent for $9 - $10 per night, $13 with electricity. Cabins rent for $40 - $98 per night.

Information: Contact Manchester State Forest, 7640 Headquarters Road, Wedgefield, SC 29168, (803) 494-8196

Poinsett State Park, 6660 Poinsett Park Road, Wedgefield, SC 29168 (803) 494-8177

Palmetto Conservation, 1314 Lincoln Street, Suite 305, Columbia, SC 29201-3154, (803)-771-0870

On the Trail

Poinsett State Park headquarters serves as the trailhead for the Wateree Passage. The 7 mile section offers the user probably the greatest variety of any passage on the Palmetto Trail. The trail offers mountainous terrain but with moss-draped trees like the swamplands along with a huge swamp. The white sands on the trail tread in places will surprise the user. It's truly a unique and exciting section of the Palmetto Trail.

Take a few moments to look around the headquarters. Built by the Civilian Conservation Corps during the 1930's, the buildings are made of coquina rock that was mined nearby. The entire area once was covered by the ocean and as shells were deposited they hardened over time to form a type of stone. The word coquina means "little shells;" however, a particularly large shell can be seen in the rock along the trail on the spillway at Poinsett.

Leaving the headquarters the trail passes through shaded woods and crosses Campbell Creek and makes a slow ascent through thickets of sparkleberry bushes. As the trail pops out of the woods, it follows Campbell Creek Road, once a railroad bed. Part of the old Willington and Manchester Railroad line, it carries the user deep into the Wateree Swamp.

The body of water to your left is Brohun Lake and was a waterway for boats moving crops down to market and supplies back up for the settlers. The shed and hand pump at the end of the road is used by hunters but the water isn't safe to drink. The trail now begins a steep climb along a sharp drop-off through beautiful hardwood trees. Take your time and enjoy one of the most beautiful sections of trail. Once in a while you will see small rocks of red sandstone along the trail tread.

Parts of the trail can be rather steep on the ascent and descent but the climb is well worth the effort. At the highest part, the elevation is over 270 feet and is one of the highest elevations in Sumter County. The view out over the Wateree Swamp floodplain and lower Richland County is spectacular. Back to your left is the South Carolina Electric & Gas Wateree Station for electric generation and in front of you is International Paper Company's paper mill at Eastover. To your far right is Cooks Mountain and on a clear day you get a faint image on the horizon of buildings in Columbia some 35 miles away.

The vegetation changes rapidly on the descent down. Hickory and shortleaf pine with sparkleberry bushes in the understory

Americorps, Shaw Air Force Base, Wateree Correction Center and numerous individuals invested thousands of volunteer hours converting the wooden trestles on the Wateree Passage into trail bridges across the swamp floodplain.

dominate the ridge but after the switchback the trees are more like those found in a cove. Water seepage from the side slope is common now and the plants are heartleaf, may-apple, trillium, occasionally bloodroot and the ferns.

The trail pops out onto the old railroad bed and makes a sharp left to continue. Back to the right along the old railroad bed some half mile is a parking area on Foxville Road. This leg of the old railroad bed would have connected to Camden. The parking area is used by hunters and fishermen and can provide an alternative access to the Wateree Passage of the Palmetto Trail.

The trail now follows the old South Carolina Railroad bed across the first two wooden trestles to connect with the old Wilmington and Manchester Railroad bed at Sumter Junction.

Prior to the War Between the States, the railroad crossed the Wateree River floodplain entirely on pilings. The railroad along with the train was destroyed in April 1865 by Union forces under General Potter. The railroad was later rebuilt using earthen causeways and eight wooden trestles.

The first trestle crosses a creek that continuously flows water due to springs up stream in the swamp that feed it. At the far end of the trestle are steps leading down to the creek for fishing access. If you listen, you will hear the sound of flowing water, an unusual sound for a swamp.

The second trestle crosses an intermittently flowing creek. Notice on the left side the remains of old pilings where the railroad branched off forming a "Y" to allow trains to turn at Sumter Junction. Just before this trestle there are steps on the left that lead down to the Warehouse Lake. In the early 1800's there was a large dock here for loading and unloading boats.

At Sumter Junction some of the old rails are still in place. You might want to check back to the left along the "Y" to where the old pilings remain in the swamp.

Trestle number 3 crosses an un-named creek which flows only intermittently. The wild hogs in the swamp like this spot to wallow and rub on the pilings. Occasionally in the distance you may see a group of wild hogs crossing the trail. They are quite shy and leave in a hurry if they sense people are present.

Beech Creek is the longest trestle and crosses the old historic waterway used for moving specially made barges. The barges were built to navigate the shallow and twisting creeks and moved cotton, lumber

The Wilmington and Manchester Railroad

In the antebellum period prior to the War Between the States, growth and prosperity was common along the Wateree River. The soils produced an abundance of crops. The rich alluvial soils of the Wateree River swamp were ideal for growing cattle and hogs with a lush growth of vegetation covering the floodplain, providing a ready food source of grazing for livestock. The rivers and creeks provided a good transportation route to the markets lower down in the state. The town of Manchester grew out of this prosperity.

Over 150 years ago railroads in the area were created with much publicity and promise to support the economic growth of the area. Cotton was king and thousands of bales of cotton from local plantations were shipped to Charleston. Lumber was plentiful and the demand was great along the East Coast. The Wateree Swamp was ideal for raising livestock and a ready market existed for the fat cows and hogs.

The first railroad built was the South Carolina Railroad, a 38 mile branch to Camden which was completed in 1848, followed by the Wilmington and Manchester Railroad in 1849. The first train arrived in Sumter in 1852. The point where the Wilmington and Manchester joined the South Carolina Railroad was known as Sumter Junction.

A "Y" track was constructed there so trains could enter the South Carolina Railroad track, back down that track, and then return to the Wilmington & Manchester line by the other prong of the "Y" track; in other words, it was a turn-around.

Middleton Depot was the principal siding for loading and unloading. Today, in the solitude of the Wateree Swamp, it's easy to imagine slow moving steam engines pulling long trains filled with cotton, lumber, and other goods or trains carrying Confederate soldiers or passenger cars filled with the families of plantation owners on their way to either Camden or Columbia. Now all this promise and prosperity lies abandoned but today it is coming to life as a great recreational experience in the form of a hiking/biking trail.

Along this section in April 1865, General Edward E. Potter and his Union army discovered nine locomotives and approximately 200 cars from the rolling stock of the Wilmington & Manchester and South Carolina Railroads. The train was loaded with munitions and supplies for the Confederate Army and had become isolated because of the destruction of trestles at other locations along the track. Potters Army's instructions were to "proceed to burn, blow up, and otherwise destroy these trains and tracks." The destruction consumed most of a day and into the night.

The explosions scattered cannon sites and mounts, cannon balls, Georgia pikes, bayonets, pieces of shrapnel, bullet molds, broken swords, and other weapons along with baggage checks, parts of seats from passenger cars and all kinds of metal objects from the train throughout the swamp. During World War II most of the remaining scrap metal from the trains was collected and used in the war effort.

Prior to the acquisition of the land by the Manchester State Forest, collectors would scour the swamp in search of artifacts. Today the use of metal detectors and removal of artifacts is illegal and punishable by fine.

The section of track from Sumter Junction to Sumter was abandoned by 1940. A portion of the track remains at Sumter Junction today. The railroad from Foxville to Wateree, originally the South Carolina Railroad line, was abandoned in 1995. About the same time a large tract of land in the Wateree Swamp containing the old rail bed was acquired by the State of South Carolina through an arrangement with the US Air Force. The state legislature provided for an additional tract of land along the west side of the rail bed to serve as a buffer for the Palmetto Trail.

and crops down to the markets returning with supplies for the planters.

The trail is now deep in the Wateree floodplain. The trees are large and the understory on the swamp floor is sparse. The soils are rich from the silt-rich flood waters up stream. The alluvial soils are soft and trees often topple over during wind storms.

A number of interesting plants have adapted to the earthen causeway. The Paw-Paw tree is common, along with dwarf palmetto, blood root, and numerous vines.

The next creek is un-named but trestles 6, 7 and 8 cross Halfway Creek and two branches of Kohler's Old River. At the end of the earthen rail bed, the trail drops off abruptly to the right side and follows the remains of the old railroad for a half mile to the Wateree River. The trail is at swamp level and allows the user to see the swamp first hand. This section floods frequently and if standing water is present users may want to delay the continuation of their trip.

A ladder arrangement carries users up to the old steel bridge over the river. The bridge has a turn-stile to allow for passage of boats; however, the bridge hasn't been opened in over 100 years.

The trail will eventually connect with the Lower Richland passage west of the river and then with the Ft. Jackson Passage.

People and Places

Sumter's Swan Lake-Iris Gardens
A Lovely Mistake

The beautiful black waters of Swan Lake form the setting for the spectacular Iris Gardens. The lake is dotted with colorful islands, and wildlife is abundant. It's the only public park in the United States to feature all eight swan species and the gardens are home to the most extensive plantings of Japanese iris. The peak bloom period is late May and features the Iris Festival. The gardens boast many other flora attractions.

In 1927 a local businessman began planning for a fishing retreat. His plantings of Japanese iris failed miserably and the bulbs were dumped into a nearby swamp. Next year the swamp came alive with blooms and since has been developed into one of the finest botanical gardens in the southeast.

There is no charge for visiting the 120 acre garden which is open to the public year-round from 7:30am to dusk.

Swan Lake - Iris Gardens
822 W. Liberty Street
PO Box 1449
Sumter, SC 29150
(803) 436-2640

Poinsett Electronic Combat Range
A Real Kick in the Pants

Poinsett Electronic Combat Range is an Air-to-Ground Bombing and Gunnery Range located about 7 miles south of Shaw AFB. This Range is controlled and operated by the 20th Operations Support Squadron at Shaw AFB. Covering approximately 12,500 acres of land near Wedgefield, South Carolina, it has been in operation since the early 1950's. In 2005 the Poinsett Range accommodated almost 2,200 combat training sorties.

It is open to the public; just sign in, take a seat on the bleachers and hang-on. The F-16's, the A-10's and various other units from throughout the southeast will put on quite a show. The range is just off SC 261 about 4 miles south of Wedgefield, SC. You need to call ahead (803) 895-2597 to check on the flight schedule of incoming planes.

The Church of the Holy Cross
A Magnificent Edifice

In the heart of the High Hills of the Santee is the Church of the Holy Cross. The church is an exceptionally beautiful example of Victorian Gothic architecture. The church was built in 1850 of an unusual

South Carolina's big rivers like the Santee, Wateree and Congaree drain water from tremendously large drainage basins. They bring silt laden waters all the way to the ocean and deposit these nutrient rich soils in floodplains called alluvial flats.

architectural design, called pise de terre or rammed earth. It's the largest complex of pise de terre buildings in the United States. Pise de terre is an ancient method of construction used as long ago as 5,000 BC by the Babylonians, and by the Chinese for portions of the Great Wall of China.

Yellow soil, earth, is pounded between parallel wood planks. The planks are then raised as the wall is constructed to the desired height. Windows and doors are inserted as needed. The walls are monolithic and quite thick. The outside of the church is covered with a preparation of lime, sand, and clay thrown on with a broom and then covered with a cement pebbledash wash and tinted with paint pigment to the desired color. This makes the outside walls impervious to water. The inside walls of the church are finished off with wooden lathes covered with plaster, tinted and scored to resemble stone blocks.

The high-pitched roof is of red tile. The interior is noted for the stained-glass windows set so as to catch the rays of the rising Sunday sun. The windows were crafted in Bavaria after the designs of the renowned Frederich Auerbach, and in the sanctuary is an Erben pipe organ from New York, installed in 1851 and one of the few working examples of this type. The church is a gem in both architectural design and furnishings.

The church is located one mile north of US Hwy 378/76 on SC 261 in Stateburg, SC. Extensive restoration work is presently on-going and the building is closed to visitors, however the grounds are open. Many notable South Carolinians from the 1700s are buried in the old church cemetery including Joel R. Poinsett.

The Sumter District has a colorful

In the heart of the High Hills of the Santee is the Church of the Holy Cross. The church was built in 1850 of an unusual architectural design, called pise de terre or rammed earth.

South Carolina's Magnificent Rivers
Geology 101

Although South Carolina is the smallest state in the Southeast, the state offers a rich variety of landscapes. The major landforms are each distinctive in their own way.

South Carolina's round-topped mountains are isolated to the extreme northwest portion of the state. Part of the Blue Ridge with elevations in excess of 3,500 feet, the forests are oak-hickory with remnants of relic species like hemlock and white pine.

The piedmont region separates the Blue Ridge from the coastal plain. Streams have cut the gently rolling hills of the region with valleys. Farm lands dot the landscape and the forests are dominated by loblolly pine that has been introduced.

The coastal plain is separated from the piedmont by a thin line of ancient sand dunes. The sands are deep and infertile. Often called South Carolina's deserts, the plants are xerophytic or adapted to the dry hot sandy soils. These ancient dunes were leveled when the ocean millions of years ago covered the Lowcountry.

The coastal plain is the largest region covering two-thirds of the state. Being nearly flat and featureless, most of the state's wetlands are located here. The rivers wind and loop across the flat sand, clay and soft limestone soils.

The rivers add much to the region's variety. From the mountains to the sea the rivers drain tremendous areas that extend well beyond the state boundaries. The drainage basins are grouped into four major river systems. They can be further classified into three types: red-water, black-water, and tidal rivers.

Red-water rivers drain water from tremendously large drainage basins. They bring silt laden waters all the way to the ocean and deposit these nutrient rich soils in floodplains called alluvial flats. Examples of these rivers are the Wateree, Congaree and Santee.

A black-water river is one with a deep, slow-moving channel that flows through forested swamps and wetlands. The term black-water describes the appearance of the water of rivers like the Edisto, the Black and the Waccamaw, which is a dark coffee color. This color results from the leaching of tannins from the decaying leaves of adjoining vegetation.

Along the immediate coast are the tidal rivers. They drain small drainages and are moved primarily by the tides. They rarely extend inland more than 30 miles. Excellent examples are the Cooper, the Ashley and the Wando Rivers.

history stretching back more than 200 years. In the 1740's, the first English-speaking settlers arrived to establish roots along the banks of the Wateree River. The "Carolina Backcountry," as it was then known, became a predominantly agricultural area. When the state capital was moved from Charleston in 1786, Stateburg, missed being elected the new capital by one vote. According to tradition, Stateburg was also considered as the location for the United States Military Academy, now at West Point.

High Hills Baptist Church
"Furman University's Roots"

High Hills Baptist Church was founded in 1772 and occupies a plot of land granted to the congregation by General Thomas Sumter. The present building, erected in 1803, is a distinctive landmark in the Stateburg area with its simple green and white painted frame structure. High Hills Baptist grew into a strong and influential church under the dynamic leadership of the Reverend Richard Furman, the pastor from 1774 to 1787.

The leadership and members of High Hills Baptist Church played an important role in the High Hills of the Santee's participation in the American Revolution. Richard Furman, an activist for the Revolutionary cause, was pursued by General Cornwallis to the point that he briefly had to flee the state. Furman later founded Furman University in Greenville, one of South Carolina's most prestigious educational institutions.

High Hills Baptist Church, located about 8 miles north of Stateburg on the road to the Thomas Sumter Tomb, today has few members and is no longer active. However, many of the Baptist congregations in South Carolina can trace their heritage to this strong and influential church.

General Thomas Sumter
"The Fighting Gamecock"

Born in Virginia in 1734, Thomas Sumter settled in St. Mark's Parish in 1767. He founded the town of Stateburg. A sawmill, grist mill, general store and a large plantation were among his financial interests. He and his wife, Mary Cantey, had one son, Thomas Jr., born in 1768.

During the Revolution, Sumter fought in numerous skirmishes and battles, including the Battle of Sullivan's Island, the Georgia Campaign, Turnbull's camp, Hanging Rock and Fish Dam Ford. His fierce revolutionary zeal had its origins in an incident involving a Captain Campbell, whose men plundered his home, placed his invalid wife in her wheelchair on the lawn and then set fire to the house. This event so enraged Sumter that he formed and led a band of guerillas in victorious combat against the British, helping to turn the tide in the War for Independence. He was known as "the Fighting Gamecock."

Following the war, General Sumter continued his public service as a member of the United States Congress. He was a staunch supporter of states rights and opposed a central government. He retired at age 76 to his beloved "Home House" in the High Hills of the Santee. He continued to actively manage his business affairs and remained a respected figure in the Stateburg community until his death in 1832 at age 98. He was the last surviving general of the Revolutionary War. General Sumter is

High Hills Baptist Church's present building was erected in 1803 and is a distinctive landmark in the Statesburg area with its simple green and white painted frame structure.

Thomas Sumter was the last surviving general of the Revolutionar War and is buried at his plantation near Stateburg, SC about 10 miles north and to the east of SC Hwy. 261.

buried at his plantation near Stateburg about 10 miles north to the east of SC Hwy 261 (just follow the highway signs).

Joel Roberts Poinsett
"The Christmas Flower"

Known as a statesman, politician and a horticulturist Joel Poinsett was born on March 2, 1779 in Charleston, South Carolina. As a well educated young person, he was fluent in French, Spanish, Italian, and German. He studied medicine, law, and military science.

His service to the United States was as Secretary of War under President Martin Van Buren and as the first ambassador to Mexico. He also spearheaded what is now known as the Smithsonian Institution. He expanded the operations of West Point and was a US Congressman.

But throughout all these endeavors, Ambassador Poinsett collected cultural and horticultural artifacts the world over. We enjoy the Christmas Poinsettias each year all because as US ambassador to Mexico he brought the plant back.

Although we remember him for introducing the poinsettia from Mexico in 1826, he did many things to advance agriculture. The poinsettia was named in his honor and the Poinsett State Park

bears his name.

He died at the age of 72 and is buried at the Church of the Holy Cross in Stateburg, South Carolina. The church is located one mile north of US Hwy 378/76 on SC 261 in Stateburg, SC. Extensive restoration work is presently on-going and the building is closed to visitors, however the grounds are open.

The Local Eateries

The community of Wedgefield may be quite small but **Battens Sportsman Kitchen** (2070 Hwy 261, 803-494-8925) offers good eats and some really friendly folks. You can get a good breakfast and a fine lunch or even a supper on your way home as well as an opportunity to thumb through the "scrap books."

Convenience Stores

Rural country stores can be really unique and **Battens General Store** (2070 Hwy 261, 803-494-8925) is no exception. Offering a big variety of supplies, food and nostalgic items from the past, you are sure to find some surprises along with all your needs.

Conner's Inc. (2480 Hwy SC 261, 803-494-5191) is a convenience store located about a mile south of Wedgefield on SC Hwy 261. They offer a full range of snacks and drinks.

Battens General Store and Sportsman Kitchen offer a big variety of supplies, food and nostalgic items from the past. Take the opportunity to thumb through the "scrap books".

Appendix

Additional outfitters, guide services & contacts.

This is not a comprehensive list nor do these outfitters offer guided trips on the Palmetto Trail itself. However, these guides may offer valuable information about the region.

1. Fisheagle Tours, P.O. Box 1086, Santee, SC 29142. (803) 854-4005 and (803) 854-2495 fax. Offers river and canal tours from Santee State Park.

2. Nature Adventure Outfitters, 1900 Iron Swamp Road, Awendaw, SC 29429. (843) 928-3316, (800) 673-0679. Offers guided trips on the Palmetto Trail.www.natureadventuresoutfitters.bizonthe.net

3. Great Wide Open Outfitters, 35 Grier St., Sumter, SC 29150. (803) 775-6103

4. The Lodge at Lofton's Landing, P.O. Box 245, Charleston, SC 29401. (803) 720-7332 and (803) 853-7586 fax.

5. Sumter Landing/Pack's Marina, Rt. 1, Box 280, Rimini, SC 29125. (803) 452-5514.

6. For local organizations and additional links, visit the SC State Trails Program at www.SCTrails.net

Suggested Reading

Able, Gene and Jack Horan. *Paddling South Carolina.* Orangeburg: Sandlapper Publishing, 1986.

Able, Gene. *Exploring South Carolina Wild and Natural Places.* Rock Hill: Palmetto Byways Press, 1995.

Bass, Robert D. *Swamp Fox: The Life and Campaigns of Gen. Francis Marion.* Orangeburg: Sandlapper, 1974.

Batson, Wade T. *The Wildflowers of South Carolina.* Columbia: USC Press, 1964.

Blouin, Nicole. *Mountain Biking South Carolina.* Helena, Mt.: Falcon Press, 1998.

Clark, John and John Dantzler. *Hiking South Carolina.* Helena: Falcon Press, 1998.

De Hart, Allen. *Hiking South Carolina Trails.* Old Saybrook, Conn.: Globe Pequot Press, 1998.

Edgar, Walter. *South Carolina, A History.* Columbia: USC Press, 1999.

Fox, William Price. *South Carolina: Off the Beaten Path.* Old Saybrook, Conn.: Globe Pequot Press, 1999.

Giffen, Morrison. *South Carolina: A Guide to Backcountry Travel & Adventure.* Asheville, N.C.: Out There Press, 1997.

Hart, John. *Walking Softly in the Wilderness.* San Francisco: Sierra Club Books, 1998.

Messmer, Catherine Campani. *South Carolina's Low Country: A Past Preserved.* Orangeburg: Sandlapper, 1988.

Rhyne, Nancy. *Tales of the South Carolina Low Country.* Winston-Salem: John F. Blair, 1982.

Sigalas, Mike. *South Carolina Handbook.* Emeryville, Ca.: Moon Publications, Inc. 1999.

Wright, Louis B. *South Carolina: A Bicentennial History.* New York: W.W. Norton, 1976.

About PCF Press

PCF Press is the publishing imprint of Palmetto Conservation Foundation. Our publications promote access and appreciation for South Carolina's natural and historic wonders. For inquiries or to order books, visit your local bookseller or our website at **www.palmettoconservation.org.**

Also from PCF PRESS....

The Waterfalls of South Carolina, Third Edition
This unique guide is an essential exploring companion for every resident or visitor to South Carolina's spectacular mountains. Packed with stunning full color photographs and easy to follow directions, this guide will take you to 31 waterfalls nestled in the rugged terrain of Greenville, Pickens and Oconee Counties.
80 pages, 32+ photographs, maps, and GPS waypoints. 6"x9" paperback.
ISBN 10: 0-974528-9-8 / ISBN 13: 978-0-9745284-9-6 $12.95

Favorite Family Hikes
The 30 walks compiled here represent a variety of trails and range of physical challenges, from strolls on the beach to mountainside scrambles. Geared toward trips for shorter legs (and attention spans) but anyone looking for a less strenuous – but still rewarding – getaway will enjoy this book, learn about wildlife, local history and neat destinations off the beaten path.
86 pages, detailed trail descriptions 6"x9" paperback
ISBN 10: 0-9745284-2-0 / ISBN 13: 9780974528427 $9.95

The Catawba River Companion
The only guidebook to the Catawba River in North and South Carolina. This book provides information on family getaways to popular destinations, maps and details on paddling trips, fishing and waterfall hikes, and recommendations for campgrounds or relaxing Bed & Breakfasts.
112 pages, maps, 6"x9", paperback
ISBN 0-9679016-8-5 / ISBN 13: 9780967901688 $9.95

101 Wild Things to do Along the Grand Strand
In this indispensable guide to the Grand Strand by James Luken and Richard Moore, learn one hundred and one wild things that you may never have known about the rich wildlife that this region has to offer. Packed with detailed descriptions, photographs and interesting trivia about local plants, animals and places, this guide gives any adventurous visitor or resident the information needed to make a wild vacation in the Grand Strand a success.
112 pages, 6"x9", paperback
ISBN 0-9745284-4-7/ ISBN 13 9780974528441 $9.95